The Early History of Roscommon County

W. E. Tudor

© Summer, 2011

Roscommon, Michigan

i

Foreword

This book is a vehicle for time travel through north-central Michigan. It focuses on the earliest days of a place that came to be known as Roscommon County. The vehicle has large windows that allow a clear view of scenes of long ago. The time travel vehicle pauses at 16 stations during the journey, the first station is just after time zero and the last ends just after the end of the 19th century. Here are the stations:

INTRODUCTION

BEFORE PEOPLE

FIRST INDIANS

HISTORIC INDIANS

FUR TRADING

BIRTHING OF A COUNTY

LANDLOOKERS & RAILROADS

LUMBERMEN ARRIVE

FIRST SETTLERS & VILLAGES

POLITICS, ELECTIONS & GROWTH

BOOM TIMES

ROSOCOMMON'S UNDERBELLY

LIFE IN THE 1880'S

NEWSPAPER REPORTS

NOT EVERYONE LEFT

SAVIOR OF THE COUNTY

Find a comfortable seat, lean back and join the journey to the earliest heritage of Roscommon County and let's learn why we have a creek named Denton, a township named Lyon, a town named Prudenville, and a road named Robinson. But even more important, learn why we are here at all just by turning a few pages....

The Early History of Roscommon County

W. E. Tudor

Introduction

Roscommon County, a 576 square mile plot of land in the north central area of Michigan, is an important part of the northern ecosystem and is, in fact, the beginning of the north woods. The outdoors environment is a critical part of life for those who live here and it is one of the attractions that draw people to the area, especially those who love wild places and wild animals including the all-important fish and game animals that fishermen and hunters revere.

The human population of Roscommon is around 25,000 people and the economy is based on tourism, a critically important generator of income for those who live and work here. Statistically, tourism rates third in income generation, following employment in education and employment by government. But it is tourism that provokes people to come Roscommon, to live here and work here. For without the tourists (including those who are part-time residents), there wouldn't be the income needed for people to live here and for the resultant teachers and government workers.

Tourists come to Roscommon County to enjoy nature's bounty. Our lakes, rivers and forests are siren calls that awaken a longing in folks for that indefinable something that causes people to endure hours of travel to visit Roscommon, perhaps for a day, a weekend, or a summer. Some spend their entire lives enjoying the pleasures that Roscommon provides: I have met people who have spent each summer of their life in Roscommon enjoying a summer-long vacation before returning to a home somewhere distant to earn a living or care for family who are obliged to live in an area where commerce of another kind is paramount.

So, what is it that brings people to Roscommon and why do they come year after year? Certainly not for farming: less than 2% of Roscommon County soil is considered prime farmland. Probably not for the weather: the lowest wintertime temperature was -48°F (February, 1918) and the warmest was 107°F (3 times in June and July, 1937) and obviously not for things that beckon tourists to other areas: mountains, seashores, architecture, museums or other man-made attractions. The specific location where people live provides a clue; during summer, the highest population density is around Houghton and Higgins Lakes. During fall, specifically October and November, the population balance shifts with a high proportion of citizens scattered about the woods and wearing orange jackets.

Thus it is indeed the physical nature of the county and all that it portends that accounts for the human interest in living and playing here in the early part of the 21st century. And so has it always been. The earliest men to arrive came In search of big game animals that were attracted by the harvest they found at the retreat of the glaciers. The earliest people were followed in successive waves by others who also found that nature provided in this place just what they needed.

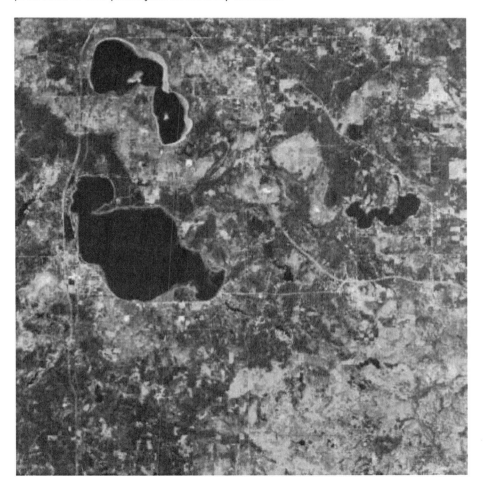

Roscommon County from 10,000 Feet

(This 2010 aerial photograph was prepared from a meld of more than 700 images that were combined using GPS coordinates to position each image correctly.)

For several thousand years, there existed a delicate balance between a small population of men and women and an ecosystem that provided the essentials needed for life for those few who wandered the trails and shores. The average rainfall of 28 inches per year was sufficient to grow fruits, berries and tubers that could be had for the picking. The streams and lakes yielded fish and shallow water plants and tubers that could be eaten raw or cooked, and the forests and meadows served as home for game that could be eaten.

When the first Europeans arrived in the state, there was no attraction for them in this wild, remote place, if they had even imagined that it existed. Instead, the natives who lived here provided the Europeans what they wanted; the skins of fur-bearing animals. A trade grew up between isolated traders and the natives who lived here. It was helpful to the natives and the traders that this place was an expressway of sorts – a stopping place in the middle of the across-state streams that provided the pathway for the efficient canoes carrying goods and furs. As fashions changed and the fur trade dwindled, Americans on their march westward became interested in owning land everyplace that offered the potential for profit. The only problem was that the land in northern Michigan wasn't for sale since the natives who lived here had little concept of the European idea of land ownership. How can you buy the air, the sky or the land, they wondered?

The matter was settled by war. The War of 1812 between the British and Americans was actually fought by a confederation of British and Indians against the Americans. The British and Indians lost. The British retreated to the north and east side of The Great Lakes and the Indians were forced to a series of treaty tables; in 1819 the eastern half of northern Michigan was ceded to the U.S. government while in 1836 the remaining western half of the state was sold by a group of Indian Chiefs. One of the Chiefs was a higher ranking Chief than many of the others. His name was Mikenauk, and other Indians deferred to him and recognized the lands in the north-central area of the state as belonging to him and his clan.

After the treaties were signed and the ceremonies were over and the liquor was drunk, nothing happened. The land remained as it had been for thousands of years, the Indians remained in their camps and the white men remained in their cities and on their farms almost as if the war and the treaty had not occurred. A decade went by and then another and another and the only evidence of the treaty signing was a thin trickle of whites passing through on their way somewhere else, somewhere more important. The only evidence that Indians no longer owned the lands in the north central area of the state was by the 'lines in the air' that certain white men drew with their chains and telescopes and papers as they tramped about the area. A whole group of men passed through the area over a period of years as the government organized survey teams to section the land and take a first look at what the government had obtained.

The State of Michigan finally took legislative action as noted in the legislative record, *"That portion of the state embraced by towns 21 – 24 north of ranges 1,2,3,4, west, shall be laid off as a separate county, to be known and designated as the county Mikenauk,"* April 1, 1840.

The legislature wasn't finished with names, however, as indicated by another record, *"The name of the County Mikenauk , as now recognized by law, is hereby changed to Roscommon,"* March 8,1843. Some white men couldn't tolerate even the name of an Indian for the land that they had occupied for thousands of years. And so the name was changed. By then, there few Indians left to protest.

At first, the new county of Roscommon also included the current county of Midland. In 1875, the two were separated and Roscommon County was finally recognized as a separate entity. The government surveyors left records of their visits and sometimes penciled names onto the lands and waters that they measured. Samuel Brink added the name Muskego Lake to his survey map. The name lasted only for a short period. Other names applied to the state's largest lake were Roscommon Lake and Red Lake. Finally, the name Houghton Lake was assigned to honor Michigan's first geologist Douglas Houghton. Roscommon's Forginson Lake was also renamed to honor another pioneer and surveyor, Sylvester Higgins, and so the county's second largest lake became Higgins Lake. The two lakes are 20,044 acres (Houghton Lake, largest lake in the state) and 10,022 acres (Higgins, the 11th largest).

Even though the land was surveyed and available for purchase in the 1850's, nobody cared. No one, that is, except the government and a few speculators who were interested in developing the area for farming or mining or for whatever else of value could be obtained. Government Interest in the area ended with the outbreak of the Civil War when the attention of all the important government officials was centered on that conflict.

When the war ended and the government offered Roscommon land at $1.25 an acre, a few brave farmers ventured into the area and began the long, slow process of coaxing produce from the land. The initial results weren't all that promising since the area was remote from any established markets. Around that time, a few savvy investors believed there was something of significant value in the county; the forests and the lumber that it could provide. Roscommon and Northern Michigan was covered in trees; oak, aspen, pine, fir, cedar and spruce to name just a few. But it was pine that attracted the most attention. Cork pine, they called it, the big pine trees with few lower limbs to blemish the straight and tall tree that was so lightweight that it floated like a cork on any of the many streams or lakes in Roscommon. The problem was how to get it. The country was so remote and so isolated that only the hardiest of land-lookers could even get a view of the riches within the forests.

Everybody knew the solution but no one knew how to pay for it. The solution was to open the area with roads and, specifically, railroads, so that travel and transport of goods to the area could be handled. Laying tracks through a remote wilderness was expensive and the railroad companies needed convincing, especially so since no one was certain if a railroad could earn a profit by running trains to and through the north woods. The government offered incentives to the railroad in one of the few ways that it could: it offered free land to the railroad providing they would build a line to the area. The Michigan Central Railroad decided to take the chance and began laying tracks north from their existing lines. By 1872 the line reached Roscommon and then headed north to the little town of Grayling, then called Forest.

The railroad ignited an economic engine that was fueled by logs. Suddenly timber men were everywhere: looking at land, speculating in land, buying lots for home sites, establishing lumber camps, supply stores, and so forth. Businesses operated at a frenzied pace. Growth was everywhere as merchants raced to supply the men and families that came to operate the camps, the mills and the transportation systems that were needed to handle the logs and lumber products. Even farmers were needed to supply grain for the horses and food for those at work in the forests and mills. The logging companies acted as if there was no tomorrow. They cut everything in sight, and sent the logs off to distant markets accessible by sailing ships and the burgeoning railroad lines.

The lumber camps became tiny villages while the county seat and village of Roscommon became a place for hell-raising by the young lumber jacks who sought a place to blow off steam. For a while, Roscommon had such a bad reputation that families on their way to Higgins Lake avoided the town altogether even though it was the most direct travel route.

As the forest began to be played out, lumber camps closed and the towns that had grown up with them faltered. For a while, there was a large push to market the cut over lands as farmland and a few unwary farmers bought the land at deep discounts. But it turned out that even cheap land wasn't enough to insure a profit as the farmers learned that much of the sandy upland soils were just not suitable for raising crops. By the turn of the century, logging had diminished to the point that it could no longer support the many businesses that had grown up with it. The population declined as businesses fell idle and then failed. Farmers and lumbermen quit paying taxes on the cut over lands and the government began taking back large parcels.

Suddenly, the very existence of the county was in doubt and efforts were begun to abolish the county government and return the idle land back to the State of Michigan for a park. The catastrophe was narrowly avoided by a far-thinking businessman who interceded with an infusion of cash that made the area once again solvent. Things improved after that and an infusion of new people came forward to replace the lumbermen.

The story of Roscommon County is too big to be told in one volume so we'll end it here, in the early 1900's after the county is saved, lumbering has moved on and the capable, industrious people of the area face new economic challenges. Those people, the grandparents of some current Roscommonites, were successful in an area that had bred them for success by the hardships of a remote area and limited technology of the times. Hopefully, this book will provide a better understanding of their lives and the challenges they faced so that we can learn and grow by knowing the things they did and what they accomplished against enormous odds.

Bill Tudor,

Summer, 2011

Chapter 1

Before People

(Roscommon in Geological Time)

Geologic time is different than regular time. You and I think about time in terms we can understand and measure. We consider the time until dinner, the time for a round of golf, and maybe the time needed for a vacation. Our sense of time is based on our experience. If we are older, we may have the sense of time for a few, or even several generations of people- several dozen years, perhaps.

Geologic time is different — it is much longer, and so long, in fact, that it is beyond human capability to imagine for most of us. Instead of events occurring in a few generations, or even a few hundred years, geologic time often marks events that required thousands and millions of years to occur. And so it is with Roscommon County. Most of Roscommon's history occurred before men ever ventured upon its soil.

The history of the county is told principally by its rocks and soils. Like many areas of the earth, Roscommon has a very old history as indicated by the age of the rocks that form the floor of the county. Roscommon's floor was built by geologic events that occurred several million years ago.

Most experts believe the earth's oldest rocks were formed 4.6 *billion* years ago, (4,600,000,000 years) as result of cooling of the underlying magma. These first rocks formed the basis of the earth's crust. The very oldest rock found that could be positively dated by radioactivity came from Hudson Bay area; it is between 3.8 and 4.2 billion years old. After the first rocks were formed, other layers of rocks were deposited in other times by natural processes and these rocks became the floor of the first areas formed. Places on the earth with very young and relatively new floors are those places where volcanoes have created new lands, the Hawaiian Islands, for example.

The processes that created the rocks generally formed three types of rocks: igneous, metamorphic and sedimentary. Igneous rocks developed from the freezing of magma, metamorphic rocks were formed by chemical and physical changes to igneous rocks and sedimentary rocks were formed by the accumulation of various sediments that were exposed to heat and pressure.

Geologists reckon time using the origin of rocks as time's markers. During the billions of years the earth has existed, many types and layers of rocks were formed and deposited on its surface. Geologists divide history into five timespans or eras; Archeozoic, Proterozoic, Paleozoic, Mesozoic and Cenozoic with the Cenozoic being the most recent. These eras are further subdivided into smaller units of time based on the layers of rocks that are found in the earth's crust. The "floor" beneath Michigan consists of a layer of sedimentary rocks from the Paleozoic era. These rocks are 14,000 feet thick and they rest on a sub floor of even earlier Precambrian rocks. These Cambrian rocks are 600 million years old.

The layer of stone under Roscommon County is Mississippian rock. This rock was deposited in the Paleozoic era about 350 million years ago. Some other areas of Michigan and elsewhere have rock floors and exposed rocks that are much younger; the Jurassic layer of stone is judged to be 180 million years old while the most recent Cenozoic era has quaternary stones that are less than a million years old. Compared to many areas, Roscommon is a pretty old place.

During the ages, Michigan's floor has lifted, fallen and turned upward in many spots as underlying volcanic activity has occurred. At times in the distant past, volcanoes have erupted and covered vast areas with igneous rock structures. At other times, a vast sea covered the rock layers for thousands of years leading to the formation of sediments and sedimentary rocks. The heat beneath the surface of the earth's crust has periodically caused the underlying molten rocks to move both laterally and up and down, leading to large stresses in the crust. These stresses and the occasional volcano have disrupted the orderly layers of rocks beneath the surface so the floor has become bent, twisted, and folded in various spots depending upon the subsurface activity. The rocks on the surface of the earth's crust have had to endure wind, rain, freezing, and the flow of water as uplifts and depressions created places where the water raged down from the heights to the lower places.

During the Mississippian era (350 million years ago), Roscommon sat at the bottom of a large but shallow sea. The sea produced aquatic life whose remains accumulated year after year, decade after decade until sediments built up. The sediments account for the deposition of shale, gypsum, dolomite and limestone that can be found in areas of north central Michigan. These sedimentary rocks built up layer after layer over the millennia that the shallow water existed.

At some point, the sea was largely drained by movement of the earth. Over time, the remaining standing water evaporated and the organic sediment became soil which hosted a wide collection of plants and animals. This furthered the deposition of organic material as these life forms died and became one with the surface matter. The Mississippian rocks contain a number of important materials, not the least of which are the deposits of oil and natural gas found in our area.

The oil and gas resulted from the anaerobic (without air) deterioration of life forms. This occurred in some low, wet areas of moist, fertile soils. These sites provided a home for primitive plants and animals and a variety of microorganisms that grew and died in these waters. After they died, they fell to the bottom and accumulated. In some places, the rocks and the water combined to provide an environment that prevented oxidation of the accumulating debris and the organic material slowly evolved into oil and/or natural gas much as occurs in garbage dumps today. Cracks and voids in the sedimentary rock beneath the bottom served as a reservoir for the liquids and gases. Pools of oil and gas have become commercially viable in Roscommon in areas where enough of the material has accumulated to make extraction economically feasible.

The most important event in the geologic history of Roscommon County resulted from a change in the weather. During one era in geologic time, for some reason, the average temperature over most of North America dropped like butter on a hot pancake. Year after year, it became colder than the year before. Winters were colder, the snow became thicker, and the snow cover lasted longer each spring. Then, during one fateful summer, the summer temperatures were cool enough so that snow cover lasted all summer. That year fall came early and brought with it more new snow. New snow covered the old layer preventing it from evaporating. By the end of that winter, the snow was thicker than it ever had been and again that summer it failed to melt. Now, the snow-covered areas reflected the sun's heat instead of absorbing it and the temperatures fell even further. The effect of the cold temperature was compounded and more snow fell. The snow layer became thicker and thicker so that the weight of snow became considerable. Finally the bottom-most snow changed. The tiny snowflakes became compressed and denser -the snow at the bottom became ice.

As the years passed the ice became thicker and thicker. After 10 years of cold, the bottom part that had turned into ice was only a few inches thick, after 100 years a few feet, but after 1,000 years, the ice had grown to the size of a small mountain. Ultimately, the ice over north central Michigan became 10,000 feet thick, higher than many airplanes fly. The huge mass of the glacier forced the ice at the bottom to press into the earth so that the glacier became like a partially buried plow. The snow at the bottom of the huge glacier that had fallen a thousand years earlier had become ice and the ice became different than that which we normally experience. Under the extreme pressure of the 10,000 foot thick glacier the bottom-most ice lost its brittleness and became something new, a hard, flowing substance with properties like plastic that forced the glacier to move. As it moved forward, it obliterated everything in its path.

As the cold continued the glacier moved southward, enveloping trees as if they were toothpicks, moving hills, pulverizing boulders into sand, scoring and gouging rocks, pushing and picking up rocks and soil and changing the landscape to a frozen wasteland.

The wasteland covered all of North America north of the Ohio and Missouri Rivers. The glacier was so heavy it depressed the surface of the earth by as much as one foot for every three feet of glacier. Both depression and rebounding of the earth under the weight of the glacier occurred slowly, taking thousands of years. (Some areas in Canada are believed to be still rebounding from the last glacier.) The glacier was not uniform in thickness, thus some areas were compressed more than others and have rebounded more than others. The nearly 200 foot difference in elevation between Traverse City and Mackinaw Island is a result of rebound from differences in thickness of the glacier in those areas.

And then the weather warmed. Instead of growing, the glacier melted and retreated to the north. This happened again and again during the periods of glaciation. The last glacier, the Wisconsin, established the current topography of Roscommon County. It lasted for 6,000 years, from 10,000 B.C. to 4,000 B.C. This glacier formed our hills and valleys, deposited our soils, and created our lakes and rivers. As the glacier advanced, rock masses were ground down to boulders and stones, basins were gouged out of rocks, soils were depressed by the weight of the ice, and stone was pulverized into sand and soil. The glacier piled debris in front of the advancing ice as it moved. When the glacier retreated to the north, piles of debris remained creating a long hill or ridge that geologists call a moraine. The leading edge moraines are not uniform because the leading edge of the glacier was not uniform; its front progressed as an irregular lobe with crevasses and tunnels due to periodic melting of portions of the ice. Moraines are scattered throughout Roscommon County, several prominent ones are south of Houghton Lake and north, south and southeast of Higgins Lake.

Other changes occurred as the glacier retreated by melting. Melting caused lakes at the edge of the glacier and ponds between the lobes of the ice front. Melt water carried with it the sand, gravel and smaller rocks that the glacier had picked up and carried with it. Where the sands and gravel were trapped between lobes of ice, hills formed that are identified as kames or kamic moraines. These structures are apparent in southeastern Richfield Township and southeastern Roscommon Township.

When the weather was warm the glaciers melted quickly and the rushing water formed rivers and streams that flowed from the melting glacier. The raging water found its way from the high areas to the lower elevations. As the rate of melting increased, the rushing water cut into the earth, creating permanent stream beds that helped drain the water. The three watersheds of our county, the Au Sable drainage, Saginaw drainage and Muskegon drainage were each formed by the glacial rivers. Each of these drainage systems sent their waters to the largest, lowest areas east and west of Roscommon; Lake Michigan and Lake Huron, also the gift of the Wisconsin glacier. The flowing water released its burden of sand, gravel and rocks to the surrounding areas. Soils developed from these fast water melts are referred to as outwash plains and they are generally mixtures of sand and gravel of uniform size.

The following sketch illustrates the irregular nature of a melting glacier and how the rushing melt water contributes to changes in the land surfaces. Lakes, rivers, hills and depressions in the surface were each caused or altered by the melting glacier as it retreated to the north. Roscommon's topography was formed by this type of glacial action.

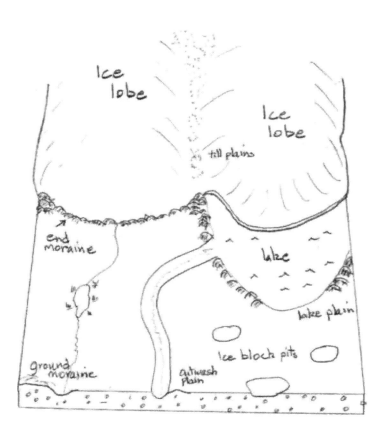

The Irregular Shape of Glaciers Created Irregular Land Forms

During lengthy periods when the glacier melted more slowly, the water released the rocks and sand more slowly. Material released in this fashion is called till, it consists of particles of varying size with the smallest sand particles having sharp edges that were not worn down by tumbling over rocks as the water flowed from the ice. Till is widely dispersed in Roscommon County and it generally is categorized as calcareous clay loam.

Parts of the glacier that were underground melted more slowly that the part above ground. When the melt water carried sand from the glacier it enveloped at least two large frozen lakes that were buried under the sand and gravel and remained isolated from the rest of the flowing water. It took years before these frozen lakes melted and the covering sand fell to the bottom. We know these formerly frozen lakes made by the glacier by their current names: Higgins Lake and Houghton Lake.

The glacier left standing water in the low spots all around the county. In fact, at least 10% of the county is covered by water. The number of lakes and ponds in the county today, more than 80, is considerably smaller than in the years immediately after the glacier melted since the process of eutrophication (the gradual filling in of ponds) accounts for many of the low flat places in the county.

Much of the soil deposited in Roscommon by the Wisconsin Glacier is sandy and is listed as well-drained upland soils. These soils are suitable only for plants that are drought resistant. The glacier also deposited some clay soils in a few areas. These areas and the low areas that have filled with muck hold water and are listed as poorly drained. These differences in soil and its water retention capability played a key role in the subsequent history of the county.

Retreat of The Wisconsin Glacier

As the ice retreated with the warming weather, the soils around Roscommon began, once again, to support life. First, the edges of ponds grew grasses and sedges as the sun-warmed water helped warm the nearby soil. Then, the upland areas began to stir with life as tundra developed in the cool, but rising temperatures. Mosses, lichens, and a thin veneer of cold-hardy grasses began to grow and fill in the barren ground. Then the animals came. The first were grazing animals searching for new grazing lands. They were giants: mastodons, giant beaver, musk ox, deer, elk and caribou who migrated northward in search of grasslands. The mastodons were the largest; they were hairy elephants that dwarfed all the other grazing animals. Then the hunters came, the first men to walk the ground that had been in gestation for a few billion years, silently awaiting their appearance.

The temperature warmed further and the soil was enriched by successions of dying plants. By 3,500 B.C. , most of the plants that we have today were emerging in north central Michigan, First were low shrubs and ferns as the temperature began to stabilize and warm. The Great Lakes were still changing, but the shape and size that we see today was beginning to emerge. Finally, trees began growing as seeds from the south were carried north on the wind. The first trees were the cold-hardy spruce: Roscommon-area forests were part of vast landscape that was nearly a single species forestland of tall spruce trees like some forest lands in Canada today.

After a long time, when the temperature had increased significantly, the spruces were succeeded by other trees and many diverse forests began to dot the county as the trees accommodated the soil and weather in successive generations to form climax forests. The poorly drained soils supported forests of cedar, birch, fir, spruce and tamarack. The sandy, well-drained soils gave birth to oak, aspen and pine. The men who had searched for wild game on the tundra became fewer and fewer and then disappeared altogether in Roscommon. Some say they moved to the north along with the ice and cold. In a short while (as measured by geologic time), a new breed of men came to replace them and Roscommon began to develop a history of people instead of just rocks and ice and snow.

Chapter 2

First Indians

The first men to tramp over the upland area of Roscommon County were Indians. In 1931, the noted archaeologist Walter Hinsdale wrote, "Houghton Lake, the largest inland lake in the state, the head of the Muskegon River, appears to have been as inviting for Indians as it is now for resorters. Within a distance of one mile from the curve in the western shore line, no less than 12 small [Indian] burial mounds were found. A group of mounds stood just west of Prudenville. Along the south beach of the lake there were at least two villages and a burial ground so extensive that the people living nearby claim that a 'big battle' must have been fought there. A group of four mounds was situated upon the north shore at the mouth of Baccus Creek or the 'Cut.'"

Since Hinsdale completed his survey work in the early part of the 20th century, scores of archaeologists have completed numerous investigations all over Michigan and the Great Lakes area. They found numerous sites where ancient Indians lived. Based on their work it is clear that Roscommon, like other Michigan locations, has been the home and hunting grounds of Indians for thousands of years. The earliest Indians came to Michigan shortly after the glaciers retreated and the newly exposed land began to support flora and fauna that could serve as food for the hungry human invaders.

Archaeologists use the name Paleo-Indians to identify the first Indians that came to Michigan. The evidence Paleo-Indians left behind is scant; after so many thousands of years virtually everything they used has disappeared, except stones. These were Stone Age men and their stone tools have survived in virtually the same condition as when they were last used.

Archaeologists have studied their tools, where they were found, what rocks and geological land forms were nearby and, by making reasoned judgments concerning the use of tools in earning a living, developed a comprehensive assessment of the people and their culture.

The Paleo-Indians appeared on the scene in Michigan about 13,000 years ago, or as archaeologists say, 13,000 years B.P. (*Before Present* times), a period when glacial ice was still melting from regions in the north and the climate was still warming. Mostly stone tools have been found to indicate the presence of Paleo-Indians but one skeleton was found in Oakland County in the south east part of Michigan; it was the remains of a person who lived 7,000 years B.P. The characteristic indicator of the presence of the Paleo-Indians is the bi-faced, fluted points that have been found at many sites around Michigan. These relics have been consistently dated to the period of 8,000 to 10,000 years B.P. These findings are consistent with other studies that show Roscommon County and the rest of the Lower Peninsula was ice free by 7,900 B.P. The Paleo-Indians arrived in Michigan shortly after the ice melted and the big game arrived to feed on the emergent plant life.

The stone points used by these most ancient Indians are virtually the same as the well-known Clovis points (named after the initial find in Clovis, New Mexico) that have been found at many sites in the West. The stone points were used as spear points for killing big game animals that appeared in Michigan; mammoths, mastodons, giant moose and beaver, caribou, musk ox, and another animal called a peccary. Archaeologists believe that the huge mastodons were a primary target; one animal would have fed many tribesmen. The mastodon was an elephant-like animal that made its appearance and disappearance during the same era as the Paleo-Indians. Since it was so large, it would have required a careful, cooperative effort among the hunters to bring down. Some evidence suggests the animals may have been driven into a swamp or bog where they would have been mired in the muck and unable to flee before they were attacked by a team of spear-wielding hunters.

The hunting of these beasts is indicated by the finding of fluted points at or near the sites where mastodon bones have been found. At one site a mastodon rib bone was found with a fluted point embedded in it. The fluted points, from 1.5 to 6 inches long, would have been used as spear points with a stick, split on the end and secured to either side of the fluted area of the stone with sinew. This hafted weapon could have been thrust into the mastodon far enough to reach its vital organs. Most relics of either mastodon bones or fluted stone points have been found south of a line intersecting Gladwin, Claire & Oseola counties although a few have been found as far north as Traverse City.

Several fluted points have been found in Roscommon County at various sites by an accomplished amateur archaeologist.*[1] The presence of these artifacts and others collected in Roscommon prove that Roscommon hosted some of the first men to live and hunt in the Great Lakes area. These Indians spent most of their time in pursuit of big game which was the largest source of their food. Since most of their permanent villages with the largest collection of stones were alongside the shorelines of the largest lakes, it is likely that the Paleo sites found in Roscommon were temporary camping sites.

\

---

[1] Private conversation with an amateur archaeologist who has searched numerous Roscommon County sites.

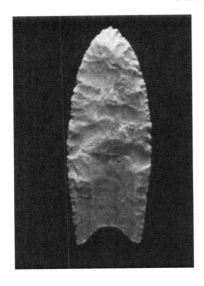 

Fluted Stone Spear Point   **Spear Point Secured with Sinew**

The Paleo-Indians were succeeded in Michigan by another Indian group that archaeologists refer to as Archaics or Boreal Archaics (Boreal refers to the boreal forests that occupied a large portion of the forests in northern Michigan during this time period). These Indians are known to have lived in the Upper Great Lakes region from around 5,000 B.C. to 500 B.C. They were different than the Paleo-Indians as indicated by the types and variety of their stone tools. They used axes and adzes (an adze is a tool similar to an axe accept that it is mounted transverse to its handle so that it can gouge out wood from a log) leading to the suspicion that the Boreal Archaics may have been the first men to develop boats by using hollowed out logs to form a dugout.

Other Indians living in the area at about the same time were the Old Copper Indians (more about them later). The hallmark of both the Boreal Archaic and Old Copper Indians is that both used new kinds of tools that had been lacking in earlier cultures of Indians.

The Archaics used other woodworking tools in addition to the axe and adze. They had scrapers, gouges, hammers and drills for woodworking while other stones were used for fishing, scraping hides for clothing and wedges for splitting bones. The extraordinary thing about the Boreal Archaic tools was that the tool makers seemed to have taken extra measures in making their tools to make them beautiful as well as functional. Although the Archaics used some chipped flint like the Paleo-Indians, many of their tools were made by chipping, hammering, and pecking the stones into shape and then finishing the tools by grinding and polishing them using other hard stones or grit as media. The result was smooth, hard tools that, although not as durable as steel tools, have a certain beauty, especially when found in the ground 5,000 years after their last use.

Like the Paleo-Indians, the Archaics were also big game hunters but they seemed to have a more diverse diet; they were gatherers and fishermen and their game animals included small game as well as larger animals. The forests were an important part of their livelihood as they collected wild foods that they found growing in the forests and open areas surrounding the lakes and streams.

They hunted with both thrusting spears (like the Paleo-Indians) but also with lighter spears that could be hurled by hand or with the aid of atlatl, a wooden rod or shaft that could be gripped at one end while supporting a spear at the other end with a cup or a notch so that the speed of the projectile could be multiplied by the length of the atlatl. The spear used with the atlatl (more accurately called a dart) improved a hunter's odds significantly by increasing both the range and speed of a throw. Fishing was also an important part of the diets of these Indians as fishhooks, stone net sinkers and other fishing tools indicate.

Their tools also included scrapers, awls and antlers used for flaking stone for the making of knives from flint and quartzite. The tools included flint blades with the tell-tale "turkey-tail" basal ends. These Indians buried their dead in pits with small amounts of tools, and sometimes powdered red ochre was placed in the pits.

Turkey Tail blades of chipped flint made by the Archaic.

Numerous Archaic tools have been found in Roscommon by a skilled amateur archaeologist. The Indians who made these tools first broke off a large piece of chert (a type of flint) by hammering the edge of a rock with a larger stone or a hammer made of antler. Subsequently the broken piece was shaped to this lanceolate shape by applying pressure to the edges using another piece of antler.

The Old Copper Indians and the Hopewell Indians made their appearance in the Great Lakes area while the Archaics were still present in many places. The Old Copper Indians first appeared in the north – where copper was found, about 2,000 years after the Archaics first made their appearance. The Hopewells came from the south and made their appearance at the end of the Archaic period, around 500 B.C.

The Old Copper Indians of Michigan were the first people in the Americas to leave the Stone Age and they may have been the first metal-workers anywhere in the world. Their homes were at various spots in the Great Lakes region although their copper mines were located in the Upper

Peninsula, Isle Royale and at several sites in Wisconsin just west of Lake Michigan. The material that they learned how to mine was pure copper that existed in veins through the rock outcroppings and at shallow depths below the surface. Archaeological evidence of old mine pits have been found with the remnants of wooden levers, birch bark buckets, stone hammers, and charcoal from spent fires. They mined the copper by heating it with fires, and then plunged cold water on the veins to fracture the rocks before finally hammering and prying the ductile copper to free it.

Once mined, the copper was hammered into shape and then significantly, it was annealed by heating to improve the toughness of the hammered shapes. The Old Copper Indians used the wrought copper as a replacement for sharpened stones. Their axes, adzes, and knives are reminiscent of tools designed for stone with the exception that many of the tools featured a tang or projection at the end of the tool to enable easy fastening of the tool into a wooden handle. The Old Copper people seem to also have been the first to have domesticated wolves as pet dogs.

A tantalizing possibility is that the Old Copper people never disappeared, that they instead moved from the Great Lakes area to points further north. This view is suggested since the northern boreal forests moved north as the period of glaciation drew to a close and the cold weather animals moved with the forests. Possibly the Old Copper Indians moved north in pursuit of the game they sought for food. Old Copper artifacts found in the north are invariably newer than those found in their southern range. The northward trail of the Old Copper Indians disappears in Manitoba between Lake Superior and Coronation Gulf after 500 B.C. Then, in 1771, a man named Samuel Hearne reported on finding a group of Indians and Eskimos who made and used copper knives, adzes, awls and arrowheads. Their tools were like those of the Old Copper Indians and they were made by cold hammering and annealing. Perhaps these were the last of the Old Copper Culture Indians that survived into the 18th century.

The Hopewell Indians were another prehistoric group who occupied parts of the eastern U. S. for more than 1,000 years beginning around 500 B.C. They were mound builders whose achievements in trade and cultural development eclipsed all prior Indian cultures. The Hopewellians entered the Great Lakes area from their homes in Ohio and Illinois and traveled along the St. Joseph River and then to the Grand River where they established an important center at the present site of Grand Rapids. Later, the Hopewellians traveled north to the Muskegon River and established homes there although they seemed to limit their homes to areas where their extensive agriculture could be pursued. They built large domes to bury their dead as well as large earthen walls of varying shapes whose purpose is still unknown.

The large Hopewell mounds were found to contain dazzling artwork – some of the finest craftwork ever produced. They made body ornaments, statues, pipes for smoking and for ornamentation, and effigies of game animals that presumably related to their religion. They made musical instruments out of wood and bone and their large burial mounds included numerous pottery pieces that were decorated.

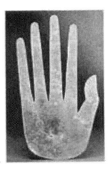

Stylistically Carved Hand (Hopewell)

Both The Old Copper Indians and The Hopewells faded into history and the active mining of copper seemed to be lost. No Indian copper artifacts from this early period have been found in Roscommon County.

The last group of Indians in Roscommon before the historic period was the Woodland Indians. The people from this group were the immediate ancestors of the tribal people found in Michigan by the first European explorers. They lived in Michigan from 500 B.C. to the historic period beginning 1600 A.D.

Archaeologists have subdivided the Woodland Indians into early, middle and late to identify some significant cultural changes of these groups. Those who lived from 500 B.C. to 100 B.C. were known as Early Woodland. These Indians were different from others who lived before them based on their use of burial mounds and pottery. Their tools were similar to those used by earlier Indians and they spent their time in hunting, fishing and gathering wild plants, fruits, nuts, berries and seeds for food as did the late stage Archaics. Their burial customs, however, seemed to be more elaborate than earlier Indians as they buried their dead in mounds and placed tools, weapons, utensils, ornaments and red ocher along with the skeleton. The skeleton or skeletons were buried in a flexed position for reasons undetermined. The burial mounds of the Early Woodland Indians were not as large as those elaborate mounds of the Hopewells.

Indians that lived in Michigan and Roscommon after 800 AD but before the historic period are called Late Woodland. These Indians may have been the earliest to use the bow and arrow. They also had learned how to fire clay to make pottery and pipes for smoking. Their pottery had rounded bottoms that were decorated with cord-like impressions on the exterior. Some of the Late Woodland Indians had extensive agriculture of tobacco, sunflowers, corn, squash and beans where the soil and climate permitted. They had dogs and more substantial dwellings made of saplings and poles pushed into the ground and covered with bark or mats of woven materials. Their arrows were tipped with small, triangular points from chipped flint.

A Collection of Indian Arrow Heads of Typical Shape

During the Late Woodland period Indians began to develop social structures based on family and extended family units that would later be called clans. The permanent villages and the clan structures prompted rules and taboos concerning many aspects of daily life. The relationships and rules of living led to the formation of associations between groups of Indians who lived in areas within traveling distance. By the time European visitors arrived, these relationships among groups led Indians to consider themselves as belonging to definable tribes or nations.

These nations of Indians were still Stone-Age people at the time of their first contact with Europeans. Europeans considered themselves superior to the natives and a conflict erupted that was to last for more than 200 years over the breadth of the continent. In fact, Native Americans were just as intelligent as Europeans and considerably more knowledgeable regards their natural environment, but they lacked technology possessed by the white race.

Europeans and their predecessors had the advantage of having lived where wild creatures existed that came to be domesticated. The domestication of these wild creatures, most notably the auroch (later to evolve into our current cow), sheep and goat, provided early man a source of food more easily obtained than by hunting. The result was that people with livestock had the luxury of time to devote to tool-making and their tools became especially useful for agriculture. One success led to another and soon those who lived across the oceans were experimenting with the manufacture of metals while American natives were living in small groups that the local supply of game animals could support. Roscommon Indians were typical of these small groups who lived in the area on and off as the hunting season allowed.

Professor Hinsdale personally observed several Indian sites in Roscommon before his 1931 book was published. He noted that most of the archaeological evidence was found around Houghton Lake. It is likely that Indians found Houghton Lake inviting because its shallow waters furnished easily obtainable food for them: fish, water-loving tubers, mollusks, rice, and game birds.

Hinsdale identified three villages: two on the south shore of Houghton Lake and one on Robinson Creek, just south of the village of Roscommon. Since Hinsdale's work, another old village was discovered along the north shore of Lake St. Helen. This site was examined by archaeology students from Kirtland College and several artifacts were found. It is likely that the Houghton Lake villages were semi-permanent, old villages based on the size of the burials and the nearby mounds whereas the Robinson Creek and St. Helen sites may have been village sites that were used only as temporary seasonal camps for hunting and gathering.

Roscommon County was clearly a locus point for Indian travel since the natives used canoes on the Au Sable, Manistee and Muskegon Rivers to travel to Lakes Michigan and Huron. In addition to canoe travel, Michigan Indians traveled by walking before horses became available during the historic period. Hinsdale found the remnants of several Indian trails in the county.

Roscommon's ancient Indians were a people on the move. The hunters traveled around the state on foot in pursuing game while the women pursued the gathering of fruits and berries. Entire clans occasionally travelled as a group for trading with other Indian groups. Pilgrimages must have been made to other areas to trade for salt, to obtain flint and other materials for tools and pottery. Additionally, Indians travelled through the forests for war and made occasional pilgrimages for ceremonies of marriage or burial.

The consequence of all this travel was the creation of trails throughout the state. The best known Indian trail in the state, The Saginaw Trail, traversed Roscommon County from north to south as it wound its way past both Houghton and Higgins Lakes. In his work before 1931, Hinsdale was able to identify large portions of the Saginaw Trail as well as smaller portions of local trails along the South Branch of the Au Sable River and a small remnant of an east-west trail just south of the village of Roscommon in an area that was previously referred to as the "Long Crossway Swamp." The trail on the north side of the Mason tract along the Au Sable appears to have been an Indian trail according to Hinsdale.

Many Indian trails meandered through the forests and many followed the course of a stream toward a lake or a favored meeting place. Some historians speculate that many of our current roads evolved from Indian trails. Those roads that are neither straight nor follow survey boundaries are often identified as having their beginnings as former Indian trails.

Hinsdale also identified Indian mounds (used as burial mounds for Archaic and Early Woodland groups) and a later burial ground presumably used by Indians from the late Woodland period. He noted a total of 19 mounds in the county.

Indian Sites in Roscommon (Hinsdale, 1931)

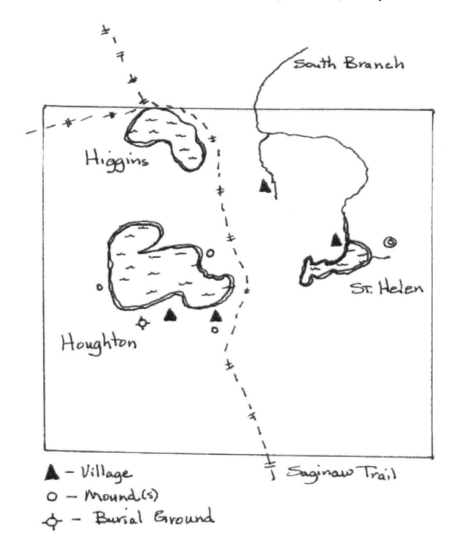

South Branch

Higgins

St. Helen

Houghton

▲ – Village
○ – Mound (s)
◇ – Burial Ground

Saginaw Trail

Prehistoric Indians also built large, earthen enclosures commonly referred to as forts, although the purpose of these enclosures has never been verified. Forts built in antiquity are located on each side of Roscommon, in both Missaukee and Ogemaw Counties. The Missaukee forts are of two types; circular and serpentine shaped. Those in Ogemaw are circular and U shaped and are located near the Rifle River. The forts must have been of tremendous importance to the Indians given the amount of energy needed to construct them since the enclosures are large, the longest serpentine being 450 feet, and the builders used only hand tools made of wood and stone.

It is clear that the first human inhabitants of Roscommon were among the most ancient of Indians based on the finding of their stone tools. Other finds demonstrate that later Indians, the Late Archaic and Woodland Indians have also called Roscommon home at least for temporary periods. Fortunately, enough studies have been conducted to lend credence to the view that we have a rich history of Indian habitation all around Roscommon County.

Historic Indians

(Historic Indians: those who lived after the first white influence until modern times - approximately 1600 to 1850 in northern Michigan)

The interior of area of northern Michigan was the homeland of Indians for thousands of years. The tribal affiliation of Indians who lived in Roscommon in the late 16th and early 17th century is uncertain since the written accounts of the earliest Europeans indicate that the borderline between tribes intersected Roscommon. To the west, the Potawatomi's held sway and to the east, a shifting conglomeration of Sauk, Menominee, Kickapoo, Miami and Mascouten tribes were present. Furthermore, as tribes moved about in response to environmental issues, the borderline of lands they considered their own shifted frequently. Adding to the uncertainty of who was where was the practice of some tribes, like the Chippewa, known earlier as the Ojibwa, to roam over large areas in search of game. The Ojibwa stayed at each location only as long as the chase was productive. During the earlier part of the historic period (1600 to 1700) the Chippewa were mainly located in the northern parts of the Great Lakes area and especially around Lake Superior.

As the 17th century dawned, Indians faced new changes that would forever affect their way of life. The changes shook the very foundation of their existence, including the place they lived. For a period of about 80 years, many of the native Michigan tribes found their homeland no longer hospitable and they left their homeland fleeing for their very lives. The changes were wrought by invaders who brought them disease, irresistible intoxicating liquors and a new kind of warfare that decimated some tribes and sent them fleeing hundreds and thousands of miles from their ancestral homeland. Paradoxically, the invaders who initiated the changes were the French traders who meant no harm and, over the long term, lived among the Indians and adopted much of their way of life.

The invaders came by ship to the shores of North America, bringing with them technologies that seemed like magic to the wide-eyed natives. No one is certain who were the first Europeans to visit the New World and its earliest Indian inhabitants. Some say Lief Ericksen and his cohorts from Greenland about 1000 A.D. while others insist on Columbus and there are even a few who say the Chinese arrived on our shores shortly before Columbus.

This much is known for certain: after the voyages of Columbus the word spread throughout Europe and several entrepreneurs made haste to get to North America. Their aim was to take advantage of the rich fisheries off the coast of Nova Scotia. By the latter part of the 16th century, Dutch ships and others were regularly filling their holds with fish. They visited the mainland before their long trip home to take on fresh water and other such supplies as the mainland environment offered. The sailors on board became acquainted with the shy natives that watched from the shore. [The sailors used the name Indians for the natives, the same name Columbus had used since he thought he had reached India].The sailors noticed the pelts that many natives wore against the cool breezes. The Indians, for their part, were fascinated by the iron tools the sailors used and a trade was made. The next fishing season, many of the sailors came ashore with many iron and copper items to trade for the soft pelts and the fur trading industry was off to a roaring start. Soon, the sailing boats were earning as much money by the fur trade as by fishing.

The trade goods brought by the Europeans made their way inland. Indians from far back in the interior first heard stories of the strange white people and the wonderful things they were willing to trade for a few furs. The trade items instantly made stone tools obsolete and the natives quickly adopted their use for daily living. The consequence of the widespread availability of the white goods is that Indians became more like whites, and, over time, those first whites who ventured far inland and away from their society became more like Indians.

The first site of regular trading began at an Indian village and trading center known as Tadoussac, a village several miles upriver on the St. Lawrence. By 1599 the French had entered the picture and one Frenchmen in particular, Samuel de Champlain, had convinced the King of France of the profit potential in the fur trade and the opportunity to capture new lands for France. The king was also desirous of finding the long anticipated route to China through the new continent and so he authorized Champlain to begin explorations to the interior lands. In 1608 Champlain sailed 130 miles from Tadoussac up the St. Lawrence River and stopped at a point of land to build a fortification for the protection of settlers that he brought along. The settlement became known as Quebec City. At Quebec and later, at Montreal, Champlain and other French began trading with local tribes of Algonquin-speaking Indians. Frequent visitors to the area were Huron (from the French word hure meaning savages). The Huron had traveled many miles downriver from the western lands in their birch bark canoes to bring furs for trade.

In 1615, Champlain decided to visit the lands of the Huron to cement relationships for the fur trade and to learn if the huge western water that they spoke of could be the ocean surrounding China or at worst, provide a path leading to China. He brought with him four clerics whose aim was to win new souls for the Catholic Church among the Huron. The Huron seemed more enthusiastic than other tribal Indians about such things and the clerics known as Recollects eagerly joined the Indians and sent back reports of things they heard and saw. Champlain thereupon set out himself for the west with native guides along the Ottawa River. Finally, on a warm afternoon in late July his canoe rounded the last bend in the river and Champlain became the first white man to gaze upon Lake Huron. He also ran into a group of Indians that the Huron guides called Odawa (traders). They were engaged in drying huckleberries for their wintertime use. The Huron guides knew these Indians well but they weren't anxious for the French to become acquainted with them. The Huron were reticent about

27

the French getting to know the Odawa since they were the suppliers to the Huron of many of the rich furs that the Huron traders carried east to the French.

After this trip Champlain sent two men to live among the Indians to further relations with them. The first was Étienne Brûlé. After living one year learning the language and the customs of the Huron, Brule traveled widely with them. Brule's success prompted Champlain to send another young man, Nicolet, on a similar mission. Both men traveled far to the west and eventually became the first of their race to visit the Upper Great Lakes. After Brule and Nicolet made their historic travels into Michigan, French religious leaders ventured into the Michigan wilderness searching for souls for Christianity among the natives. In 1641, Fathers Isaac Jogues & Charles Raymbault arrived at a village of 2,000 natives along a wide river in the north separating Lake Superior and Lake Huron. They named the place Sault Ste. Marie after the rapids that contained the plentiful whitefish. Other clerics and traders soon followed including Father Jacques Marquette in 1668 who established a permanent mission to serve the natives. Sault Ste. Marie thereupon became the oldest city in the Northwest Territory and one of the oldest in North America.

The first European to visit an inland area of northern Michigan was Henri Nouvel, another Jesuit priest who was a contemporary of Father Marquette. The Jesuits assigned Nouvel to minister to the Indians at the Sault. A visiting band of Chippewa invited him to spend the winter with them and Nouvel agreed. The group traveled down the coast of Lake Huron and up the Saginaw River where they landed on a point of land now called Chippewa Island in the present city of Saginaw. After making the arduous journey, the Jesuit priest climbed out of the canoe and offered a prayer for their safe arrival to this inland point that was hundreds of miles from the outpost mission at the Sault.

From the writings of the clerics and explorers who first arrived in the north woods, we have a somewhat hazy picture of Indians in northern Michigan. The Huron, a tribe well-known to Champlain were relatives of the Iroquois, the tribe that made their homes south of Lake Erie and Lake Ontario. The

Odawa, friends of the Huron lived on Manitoulin Island, The Potawatomi, those who occupied all the western part of the Lower Peninsula while the Saulters (Ojibwa) occupied all of the Upper Peninsula and were periodic visitors to Mackinaw. The eastern half of the state was occupied by a number of tribes; The Sauk, Fox, Kickapoo, Menominee, and Mascouten.

Simon Pokagon (1830 – 1899)

Probably the best known Indians of the Potawatomi tribe were father and son Chiefs, Leopold and Simon Pokagon. Simon was educated; he attended the University of Notre Dame and Oberlin College. Simon was a visitor to the Roscommon area. He spoke of camping at the headwaters of the Manistee River in 1850 while engaged in the fur trade.

Indians from the eastern seaboard to the Upper Great Lakes where all affected by the fur trade. All wanted the trade goods and the liquor that the white men offered. Those tribes who lived in the most advantageous position for the trade became the objects of hatred for those who were disadvantaged either by distance, problems in transporting goods, or worst of all, by the lack of good will and confidence of the French traders. The Indian practice of warring with their neighbors was given a sudden and dramatic impetus. The flames of hatred were further fueled by competition among the whites in obtaining the best furs at the lowest prices.

The Dutch and their allies, the Iroquois, were jealous of the high quality furs being provided by the northern tribes to the French along the St Lawrence River. The Iroquois, urged forward by the Dutch businessmen who provided them with the first firearms ever seen in the New World, began a campaign of extermination aimed at the major French trading partners. The fighting that erupted across the entire north began and was to last for 80 years, The Beaver Wars. The Huron were a major casualty of the Beaver War when the Iroquois exterminated entire villages of Huron, killing all within. The Huron, unable to withstand the repeated sieges by the Iroquois even with their stockade villages, left their ancestral homes and moved west into Michigan. Their friends and trading partners, the Odawa followed them. Of course, Michigan was already occupied. The movement west caused a cascading issue affecting numerous other tribes and panic set in leaving much of the interior of Michigan empty.

The Beaver Wars are considered one of the bloodiest series of conflicts in the North America. The Indian practice of killing all their enemies including defenseless women, children and old people led to panic among those who were in the path of the ruthless Iroquois. A measure of peace was finally restored in 1701 in Montreal by 39 Indian chiefs, the French and the English. In the treaty, the Iroquois agreed to stop marauding and to allow refugees to return to their homeland. The Potawatomi returned to Michigan, however, they returned only to the southern part of the state; those who left Roscommon and the central area of Michigan never returned to their homeland. The Odawa returned from Green Bay and paddled across the lake and made new homes on the east side of Lake Michigan at a place called L'Arbe Croche (crooked tree) near and around

Cross Village. Those of the Huron who survived the onslaught of the Iroquois never returned to the east side of Lake Huron; they relocated at several sites in Michigan and northern Ohio where they became known as Wyandottes for their home along the Wyandotte River.

The Ojibwa (or Chippewa) was the largest tribe in the Upper Great Lakes area and they lived all around Lake Superior. Their language was Algonquin, a French word that was taken from the name for a small tribe in Quebec. The name Algonquin was used to describe all those Indians with similar language who were probably related in earlier times. The tribes who spoke the Algonquin language or a version of it were the Ojibwa, Odawa (or Ottawa), Potawatomi, Menominee, Miami, Passamaquoddy, Sauk, Mascouten, and at least 28 others. Those underlined lived at one time or another in northern Michigan and may have lived for some periods in the Roscommon area.

The nomadic Ojibwa of the north (hereinafter identified as Chippewa) joined in the relocation of Indians in Michigan with many moving south from their ancestral homelands of the north. As they moved south, they encountered other tribes who contested their right to move on land they felt was their own. The famous Grayling-area Chippewa Indian David Shoppenagon (1812 -1911), said that his father fought a battle with the Huron who lived along the Au Sable River. Bands of Chippewa were able to summon their kin from other areas when conflicts arose. One such confederation of Chippewa and Odawa (now known as Ottawa) attacked a large Sauk village at their homeland along the confluence of the Tittabawassee, Shiawassee, Bad River and Swan Creek. Most of the Sauk were slaughtered; the few survivors were driven from their village and sent west. Here is an abbreviated account from the Bay City Journal edition of March 16, 1885.

To Editor of the Bay City Journal:

Dear Sir:

"My father immigrated to the Saginaw Valley when I was but ten years old, and although my locks are turning gray, it seems as if it was but yesterday. But what a change has come over our beautiful valley! Then it was one vast wilderness, and nothing disturbed the waters of this beautiful river save the Indian and his canoe.

I was accustomed for many years to travel up the different tributaries of the Saginaw and on nearly all I found indications that the Saginaw Valley was inhabited by a different race of people prior to the present Indian. On most of the tributaries can be found mounds filled with human bones, which I have often opened for my own satisfaction, and found them lying in all positions showing that they were thrown together without any regularity, and satisfying me that they were killed in battle. This awakened in me an interest to find out who they were, how they came there and what became of them. I often questioned the Indians in regard to it, but they would invariably say, that there were two or three very old Indians living on the Bay shore, who could tell me about it and gave me their names.

Accordingly, on one of my journies to the Bay, I sought out and found one of these Indians in question. His name was Pu-tea-quas-a-min. I had often heard of him before as a traditionalist or historian — one that had the history of his nation. He was a very old man — the most so I ever saw. I asked him his age. He said

"My son I am very old; I am a great deal over one hundred."

I told him that it was said he could give me the history of his race. He said he could as it was handed down to him by his grandfather who was older than he was now when it was told to him.

He said the Socks occupied the Saginaw River and all its tributaries, extending from Thunder Bay on the north to the headwaters of the Shiawassee on the south, and from Lake Michigan on the west to Detroit on the east. The balance of southern Michigan was occupied by the Pottawatomies. The Lake Superior country was inhabited by the Chipeways; the Monominees were at Green Bay; and the Sioux occupied Minnesota.

32

The Socks were always at war with the neighboring tribes. At last a council was held, consisting of the Chipeways, Pottawatomies, Otowas, and the Six Nations of Canada and New York, at which it was determined to exterminate the Socks.

At a given time, they all met at the Island of Mackinaw. There they fitted out a large army, and started in bark canoes, and proceeded south until they reach what is now called Otowas Bay. They then divided the largest part of the army proceeding up the west side of the Bay and landed in the night at Petobegung. The other part of the army cruised to the Charity Islands, and from there to the east shore of the Bay, at a point near the mouth of the River. It was arranged that both armies should land at the same time. That on the west side of the Bay left their canoes, and proceeded at night on foot, and attacked the main village, and massacred nearly all the inhabitants. Those who escaped retreated in canoes, some to Skull Island, and others across the River to another village. Here they were met by that part of the army that came up on the east side of the Bay, and a desperate battle took place in the vicinity of the present residence of W.R. McCormick, that being the highest land, where they fortified themselves, and where at the present time can be found the remains of those said to have been killed in that battle. Here they were again defeated. They then retreated to Skull Island, where the others had already gone. Skull Island is a little island next above what is now known as Stone Island. Here they considered themselves safe, as their enemies had no canoes, and they could fortify themselves. – But next night after their retreat to the Island, the ice froze thick enough for the allies to cross, which they did, when an indiscriminate slaughter ensued. They were all exterminated, with the exception of twelve families.

The allies then divided, some going up the Cass, some up the Flint, others up the Shiawassee, Titabawassee, and so on, where there different bands located. But the largest battles on any of the tributaries were fought on the Flint. One occurred about half a mile below the present village of Flint on the bluff, where there are over seventy mounds at the present time. There was another fought about a mile above what is now the village of Flushing, on the farm formerly owned by a Mr. Bailey. Here there are also a large number of the mounds, which show that a disparate battle was fought. The last battle on the Flint, was fought about fourteen miles below Flushing, on farm formerly occupied by the late James McCormick. There was also a heavy battle fought at what is now called the Bend of the Cass, or Bridgeport Center. This place was regularly fortified, and it is not more than twenty-five years since these fortifications could be distinctly traced. They occupied about five acres. The next battle of any consequence was on the Titabawassee on what has since been a farm occupied at one time by James Fraser. The difference between this and the other battle grounds is that the slain were all buried in one mound.

After the Socks were all exterminated, with the exception of the twelve families before mentioned, a council was held to determine what to do with them. It was finally agreed to send them west of the Mississippi, and an arrangement was made with the Sioux that no tribe should be allowed to molest them, and the Sioux should be responsible for their protection, which agreement was faithfully kept.

The Chipeways being the most numerous (of the conquerors) that language eventually predominated, but at the present time, the Indians in the Saginaw Valley do not speak in all respects the same as the Chipeways on Lake Superior from whom they originally sprang. The mixing of the different nations in the Saginaw Valley is the cause of it.

Pu-tea-quas-a-min say his grandfather told it to him, when he was a boy which must have been ninety years before, and that it had been handed down to his grandfather by grandfather when he was a boy, and so on, from generation to generation."

Skull Island alluded to above, derived its name from the number of skulls that remained on it for years and years after the massacre.

Pu-tea-quas-a-min, from whom the above tradition was obtained, died in the year 1834, on the Cass River, and was said by the Indians to have been one hundred and twenty years old.

The Indians who lived in and about Roscommon in historic times were members of either the Chippewa or Ottawa tribes. These two nations and the Potawatomi in the south shared a common language, and other cultural similarities. For a period, there was a confederated council of Indians who represented the three tribes and they referred to themselves as The Three Fires. Indians from any one of the tribes were comfortable living close of each other and sometimes they lived together in villages with a single Chief.

A Chief was the leader of either a tribe or a clan. During periods of war, both a war chief and a 'political' Chief were the headmen for the group. Clans were smaller groups of Indians, often only a few extended families who lived together and moved about as a more or less uniform group under the leadership of a single Chief.

The Indian Chief forever associated with Roscommon was Mikenauk, a high ranking Ottawa Chief who may have used Roscommon as a winter hunting ground during the early part of the 19th century. It is likely that Chippewa also lived in the area, in which case, Mikenauk would have been the ranking Chief. Little is known of Mikenauk beyond his signing of the 1836 treaty of Washington. The treaty language indicated Mikenauk's permanent Ottawa home at the time of the treaty was at Grand Traverse.

The culture of the three dominant Michigan tribes was similar in many ways and also similar to other Indians in the Northwest Territory.

Clothing – men and women wore animal skins. Until contact with Europeans, they wore only deer skins, tanned with deer brains, then cut and laboriously sewn by women of the tribe. This attire provided the standard clothes for all men and women.

Men wore breechcloths, a narrow strip of leather worn between the legs and then over a belt in front and behind and long enough so that the material draped over the front and rear of the wearer. In the warmer months, this was the only clothing worn by men and some clans even omitted this clothing. In colder weather, the men wore a shirt and leggings;

a sort of sleeve worn over each leg and tied to the belt. The shirt was long, extending to the bottom of the breech cloth. In the winter, men and women both wore fur robes with the fur side turned in over their deerskins.

Women wore dresses made of deerskins. Some clans had a standard style of over the shoulder dresses that extended to knee length as well as leggings, while with other clans the females wore skirts but were bare above the waist. Females wore their hair loose, braided or tied in a loose top knot. Men generally preferred shaved heads or mostly shaved heads with a single 'top knot' of hair that was braided to fashioned into a tight knot, often adorned with one or more large feathers and/or beads. Men from all the Michigan tribes avoided facial hair. They thought the European practice of beards and mustaches disgusting.

Both men and women wore 'dress-up' clothes for ceremonial occasions. Women adorned these garments with extensive beadwork and other decorations that were important to the tribe. Eagle feathers, bear claws, shells and colored stones were frequent adornments for their ceremonial garb. Men were more attracted to this finery than women and they proudly wore their best clothing on many occasions. Many of their adornments were intended to show their prowess in hunting and battle.

David Shoppenagon in His Best Attire

Chiefs -all three of the Michigan tribes had a similar social structure in which a respected man was named as Chief for his clan. Chiefs were chosen by their people. Although sons often succeeded fathers, such was not required and sometimes the tribe selected a respected member who was wholly separate from a chief's family. Aged Chief's also lost their role as their physical and mental powers waned. Both War Chiefs and Civil Chiefs reigned during periods of active warfare. The War Chief position was effective only for the period of conflict. Councils of the leading men were often convened with the Chief leading discussions to decide matters of great importance such as village moves, warfare, etc. A Chief's power was limited and an individual could decide to follow the Chief's decision or strike out on his own as he determined what was best for his family. A

Chief often provided assistance to those in his clan who needed help. Families and clans practiced a communal lifestyle with group support for those in need as directed by the Chief with the assent of the leading men.

Warfare- Indians engaged in periodic warfare. Their battles were most often with neighboring tribes from whom they had suffered some slight, either perceived or real. Feuds were long-lasting and involved periodic and repeated invasions. Young men gained status via warfare so that raids were often a desired undertaking. One cause of warfare was infringement on one another's hunting grounds. Indian tribes and bands were migratory, moving from one area to another within a broad range of territory that they called their own. They moved often as they consumed the available resources such as firewood, bark for canoes or their wigwams, or other essential natural materials. Movements that infringed on another tribe's land would be just grounds for a raid by the young men that might lead to a prolonged war.

Raids occasionally resulted in the taking of prisoners. When prisoners were taken they were either immediately killed or held captive until the raiding party returned home. If the captive survived the return trip he was subjected to the most extreme forms of torture that his captives could imagine. The treatment of prisoners was cause for a celebration by the entire village who delighted in the pain of the prisoner. The treatment of a prisoner often began by running the gauntlet, a long line of villagers who delighted in hitting the prisoner with a stick or a war club while the captive ran for his life. After the gauntlet and the prisoner's recovery, the torture began in earnest. Pulling out a captive's fingernails was often used to insure pain and was the beginning of a process that sometimes lasted days and involved a wide variety of mutilations before the death of the prisoner. Burning at the stake was felt to be the most painful method of execution and so it was often used as the final step.

Raiders who captured prisoners but were unwilling to take them to their village often used scalping as the means to prove their prowess in battle. Scalping was unknown by the first Europeans who explored the Great Lakes, but they learned quickly and soon became as adept as Indians in lifting scalps of their enemies. Indians also took hands, fingers and other body parts of their enemies to carry home to show their successes. Scalping became much more common with the introduction of steel knives and the encouragement for it by whites, when it was beneficial for them. Anthropologists who have studied Indian cultures have never satisfactorily explained the extraordinary, mind-numbing cruelty practiced by the tribes in warfare. Oddly, numerous accounts have been published showing that those who practiced such terrible cruelty to prisoners also occasionally offered extraordinary aid and support to complete strangers in need.

Indian view of property – Great Lakes Indians had a detailed understanding of the value of property in its essential character for supporting their lifestyle. They understood precisely which lands had waters that provided fish, mollusks, and water-loving plants used for food, and so forth. They knew which lands harbored deer, where beaver could be found, where chert was available for their tools and the like. All of these things were essential for the survival of a clan or an entire tribe. They learned quickly the whereabouts of another tribe if they happened to intrude on their homeland and such incursions were not tolerated. Property that Indians viewed as theirs was theirs alone; no other tribe was permitted without the agreement of the owners.

This view of ownership was based on the tribal rights, not individual rights. Indians in a village understood the boundaries of their property that was owned in common by all members of the village. The property owned in common was designated for use by all tribal members for fishing, hunting, gathering and so forth. Individuals did not own land, rather tribal members decided which areas of a garden, for example, would be used by which family for cultivation. The concept of individual ownership was unknown and Indians pleaded innocence of the concept when Europeans wanted to own Indian lands. They asked whites how it was possible for anyone to own the land, the air, the water or the stars.

Daily Living –Females (Indian squaws) did much of the mundane work of the household; tending the fire, preparing the food, tanning the skins, making the clothes and moccasins, cultivating the corn and carrying household goods during moving. Men spent their time in hunting and gathering, playing games, trading, and meeting with tribal leaders to decide matters of importance for the tribe and traveling in search of new homes. This division of labor was very important to the Indians. Attempts by whites to introduce farming to the tribesmen invariably met with failure as the white tutors failed to understand that squaws would belittle any Indian man who became involved with farming since the squaws saw such as actions as a threat to their place in society.

Hygiene in handling and preparing food was not a part of Indian life. A dog's tongue was equal to the task of cleaning bowls and washing and bathing was not part of daily life. Certain ailments were common among the people, especially pulmonary diseases and blindness that were exacerbated by the nearly constant contact with smoke from their campfires. Based on the few studies that have been completed, the death rate for infants must have been nearly 50%.

Indian attitudes towards whites were often ambivalent whereas white people were more often universally hostile toward Indians. The prevailing attitude among whites was that Indians were lazy, immoral, dirty, crude, brutal, and untrustworthy. Many whites believed that Indians were a less advanced form of human life compared with white people. Indians did not have similar attitudes towards whites.

Numerous instances occurred where Indians provided aid to whites who were in distress. The Indians involved in these instances seemed to feel that individual white people deserved respect and were of equal intellect to Indians but they failed to understand Indian lifestyles and were ignorant of life skills needed in the forest. Indian families routinely adopted white children that had been captured and provided loving homes for them for a number of years, sometimes for a lifetime.

In contrast to those attitudes toward individual whites, Indians believed the nation of Americans were invaders, intent on stealing Indian lands. During war, they had no remorse in subjecting captured Americans to the worst possible depredations. The cultural divide between the two groups was so wide that neither was able to avoid war.

Indian boys were subjected to training by several adult males in the tribe. Father and uncle were the main teachers but the local Medicine Man who was part doctor and part religious leader also provided training for boys. Not only did boys learn the many skills needed to survive in the woods alone, they also learned the rituals and tribe's history that was handed down through generations. A boy's graduation into adulthood was marked by a ceremony in which a boy around the age of 13 was encouraged to have a solitary dream experience. During this experience he adopted a totem, an animal that became his life-long protector. This experience required boys to leave home and spend time alone at a particular isolated spot that was of significance to the tribe. While alone without food or shelter, the boy was encouraged to sleep and dream and, if he were lucky, a vision of an animal would appear to him.

Indian girls were trained by mothers, grandmothers, and aunts on an ongoing basis. In contrast to boys, the training for girls was probably not recognized as such since girls began working with their mothers, sisters, and extended families at an early age. Their work was carefully supervised and they often learned by doing as the generations of women worked together and talked while they worked, providing the means for lightening the burden by comradeship.

The veneration of Indians toward their spirit-symbol is indicated by their practice in signing documents. Since they couldn't write their names, their practice was to indicate their name by drawing a picture of the guardian animal that they felt was synonymous with their name, be it a turtle, eagle, snail or fish of some sort. Mikenauk would have signed his name by drawing the symbol of a turtle. The Indians who signed the 1819 Saginaw Treaty each signed in this manner. These symbols were particularly venerated by the Indians as they figured prominently in the traditions about the origins of their tribe.

The word Mikenauk means turtle. The turtle was an especially respected totem among the tribes and some Chippewa clans believed they had descended from a spirit turtle. The Chippewa word for turtle is spoken with the identical sound as the word Mackinaw. It is likely that Mikenauk and Mackinaw were the same word in the Chippewa tongue. Henry Schoolcraft named the county we know as Roscommon *Mikenauk* after the Chief. Schoolcraft must have known that Mikenauk claimed the Roscommon area as his own.

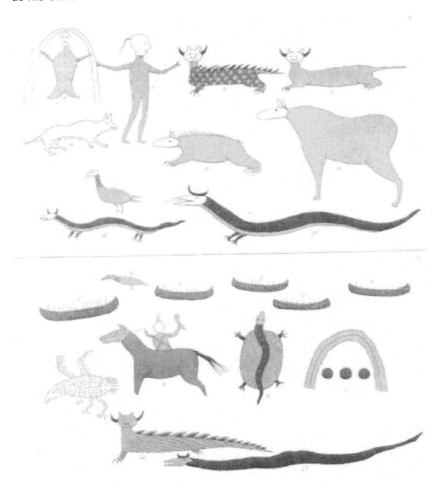

Native Pictograph on a Lake-side Rock Describes a Voyage (Note turtle)

Tobacco was a great medicine for Michigan Indians just as it was for most tribesmen in other areas. They smoked it, sprinkled it on the ground and used it in many ceremonies. On all occasions of solemnity, smoking was part of the ritual. A lit pipe was passed from chief to chief and thence to leading men with great deference as to rank. No important decision was reached or bargain was made that was not 'sealed' by smoking of the pipe, oftimes using a ceremonial pipe that was especially made and cared for and used only for important purposes.

Corn was the nearly universal food staple for Michigan Indians during the historic period. Indians had many recipes that were based on corn that was boiled and flavored with meat and/or maple sugar. Not all tribes cultivated corn, but it was commonly traded among tribes. Saginaw Indians had hundreds of acres under cultivation and there is ample evidence of corn being cultivated in many parts of the state including regions further north than Roscommon.

Corn was one of the few provisions that Indian hunters carried while they were on the chase. Here is a description of an Indian hunter from an early European writer.

"His black straight hair falls to his shoulders, his dark eyes, high cheekbones, bronzed skin, and slender but musculature shape makes him a formidable figure. His clothing is all animal skins and he has bare shoulders and arms, leggings, moccasins, breeches that cover his hips, and a long shirt, nothing else to defend him from whatever weather happens while on his long venture through the wilderness. He carries a bow and arrows, a flint knife, arrow points, thongs, a stone hatchet, his fire starting tools, and a few provisions all carried in a bag that swings from his shoulder. When traveling, he eats two meals a day if he has the leisure and is fortunate in his chase for game."

The Chippewa were largely nomadic hunters. Generally each band roamed a large area which belonged to the band for their hunting. In fall, each band separated into family units and each unit hunted in a separate area by using a bow and arrow, snares, and traps. The take needed to support them was prodigious: in the winter of 1670, a band of Chippewa took 2,400 moose using only snares. In summer, the family joined with others, usually at a fishing site, to catch fish with hooks, nets and spears. At some places like the Sault, the fish were so abundant that families could live there the entire year. The Chippewa in the north depended mostly on game for their food but they also raised corn where they could and traded for it otherwise. Many Chippewa who planted corn in the north harvested and ate their corn while it was green since the climate didn't allow the type corn they had to ripen completely. Spring meant maple syrup and families would gather to spend weeks collecting and boiling syrup. Their houses were designed to be easily disassembled and moved. Women carried rolls of birch bark that could be unrolled over saplings that were pushed into the ground to easily construct a house in an afternoon. Roscommon Indians traveled via birch bark canoes. In winter, travel was via snowshoe.

Chippewa Wigwam with its Birch Bark Exterior

Roscommon Indians used utensils that were carved from wood although they used their fingers mostly at mealtimes. They had vessels for food preparation also made of wood as well as bark baskets and pottery of fired clay. They carried food in sacks made from leather and they used a variety of tools. Both men and women used knives, scrapers and drills. Both men and women made their early tools from chipped flint while pieces of bone were used for needles and awls. After the contact period many of the early tools became obsolete with the availability of the more durable steels that the white man possessed.

The social organization of the Chippewa was largely a democratic structure where each family could make the major decisions concerning their hunting locations, etc. There were clan and band chiefs, but their power was limited. The society was patrilineal, a daughter left home to become a part of her husband's family. The religious leaders of the Chippewa were its medicine men – the two functions were believed to be essentially the same for most Indians.

The Odawa & Potawatomi were culturally similar. They were more sedentary than the Chippewa and relied more on farming and gathering for their food, although, like the Chippewa, they separated into family units for their winter hunting grounds. Polygamy was common for those successful and ambitious hunters who could support a large family. A boy was reared not only by his birth father but also by his uncles from both his father and mother. A girl was raised more by her mother although her aunts had a large measure of influence as well. Indian children often referred to their aunts and uncles as Mother and Father.

Michigan Indians were widely scattered. Just prior to contact period of 1600 A.D. there were likely no more than 15,000 Indians in all of Michigan. Villages were typically based on one or two clans with a large clan consisting of perhaps 20 families totaling 150 people when the extended family of grandparents and children were included. The Indian villages in Roscommon, if they were typical, were likely of this size. Since Indians were frequently on the move, the population of Indians in the county probably varied from season to season and year to year.

Many clans made seasonal moves from main village in the summertime to fall and winter hunting grounds followed by spring rendezvous' with other families for maple sugaring. Based on the finds made by a Roscommon amateur archaeologist, it is probable that many Roscommon Indians lived here in temporary camps as well as the village sites mentioned earlier. The Indians who lived in Roscommon would have been like those who lived elsewhere in Michigan; with the arrival of the whites their lives changed forever as they sought to improve their lives by obtaining the trade goods the whites offered.

Fortunately, Michigan Indians had just what the Frenchmen wanted – furs. And Roscommon was ideally suited for the fur trade since it sat at the intersection of two rivers that were important for cross-state travel.

Chapter 4

Fur Trading

Roscommon area Indians were influenced by the fur trade just as Indians everywhere else around the Great Lakes. The trade became their chief preoccupation apart from the basic essentials of life. The reason was simple – the fur trade was their only means to access the new technology that was suddenly available -- a technology that provided a sudden leap from Stone Age to a new era. The new goods provided comforts that were previously unimaginable - especially the all-important whiskey. Whiskey became an undeniable elixir that Indians, both men and women, found irresistible.

Michigan Indians were involved in the fur trade for two hundred years. From 1650 to 1850 the economy of the north woods revolved around beavers and other fur bearing animals. Before the French arrived, the most valuable animals to the Indians were those used for food: white-tailed deer, fish, turkey and freshwater mussels which counted toward a large part of what they had to eat. These animals had supported native human communities for ten thousand years. But after 1650 beaver was king.

The reason was simple: In 1650 people living in America and Europe worked outdoors. Only a few went to work in an office or a shop, most spent all day outdoors, likely farming or doing other outdoor jobs in good weather and foul, enduring all that nature delivered. Of course, one of the essential things required to withstand inclement weather was a good hat. And beaver made the best hats.

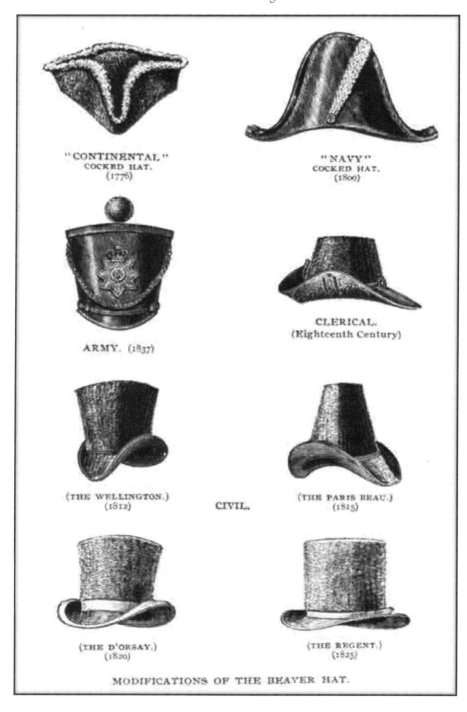

"CONTINENTAL"
COCKED HAT.
(1776)

"NAVY"
COCKED HAT.
(1800)

ARMY. (1837)

CLERICAL.
(Eighteenth Century)

(THE WELLINGTON.)
(1812)

CIVIL.

(THE PARIS BEAU.)
(1815)

(THE D'ORSAY.)
(1820)

(THE REGENT.)
(1825)

MODIFICATIONS OF THE BEAVER HAT.

Because beaver fur is waterproof, beaver skins could be shaved and pressed into a pliable felt that kept the wearer both warm and dry. From Russia to the Riviera and across the American colonies, the preferred hats were made from beaver. In Europe especially, it became a mark of prestige to wear a hat made from the nearly indestructible fur of the lowly beaver.

Europeans had been wearing hats made from beaver felt for years. Chaucer spoke of beaver hats in the Canterbury tales in his 14th century piece, and others note that felting process had been known commercially since Augustus Caesar. In any case, beaver was a preferred hat-maker's raw material that had come in short supply just as North America was being discovered. Europeans had exhausted their supply of native beaver and the hat-makers were desperate for new sources.

The market for beaver skins was huge. Suppliers of beaver skins could grow rich as the hat makers in England and elsewhere were willing to pay large premiums for the beaver skins they used to make hats. As a result, merchants in Montreal imported products that Indian hunters wanted, and demanded beaver skins in return. Imported trade goods included metal knives, awls, and kettles, steel flints for starting fires, guns and ammunition, whiskey (which, though officially prohibited, was supplied steadily through the black market), woven woolen blankets, and porcelain beads for jewelry. These trade goods were shipped into the interior for storage in regional warehouses in settlements such as Michilimackinac, Detroit, and at other trading centers. The profit potential was enormous, as much as 600 to 700% for the traders when fur was in demand and no major disasters occurred, such as the loss of an entire shipment of trade goods during the perilous trip from Montreal to Michigan.

In the fall, traders would advance guns, ammunition, and other supplies to Indian hunters on credit, and in the spring the hunters would return to pay off their bills in furs-a system that kept most Indian hunters in permanent debt to their French employers. The traders would pack large canoes with thousands of pounds of pelts for the trip back to Montreal, and beavers caught in Roscommon would end up on the heads of customers in Paris or London. Military garrisons were established throughout the Great Lakes to make sure that trade goods came in and pelts went out with as little interruption as possible.

For most of the eighteenth century, furs came steadily from the tributaries of Lakes Michigan and Superior, especially Michigan, Wisconsin, Minnesota, and western Ontario. The first to control the trade were the first explorers of the Great Lakes region, the French. Ultimately, they were superseded by the British after the end of the French and Indian war of 1763. Under the British, who controlled the trade even after the American Revolution, Indian hunters from the Great Lakes areas provided a major source of income: in 1767 a third of Mackinac furs came through Green Bay. American fur traders came to ascendance after the War of 1812 and after John Jacob Aster ruled the trade from his post on Michilimackinaw.

The first trader to come to Michigan was Jean Nicolet, he who was sent by the Frenchman Samuel Champlain to explore the west. Nicolet was a trader, and he spent the rest of his life after his travels through Michigan trading with Indians from his home base along the French River in Canada. After Nicolet wandered around northern Michigan, there came hordes of lawless Frenchmen, those who evaded the law that required licenses to trade. These men were generally unlettered and left no records of their travels and their places of business in the back country of Michigan.

One of the early recorded trading ventures was completed by two Frenchmen who were educated, Medard Chouart, and Sieur de Groseilliers, who came to the Sault and spent the winter of 1659 there. They returned to Quebec with 60 canoes loaded with furs. Another famous Frenchman, LaSalle, brought a group of 25 Frenchmen to Michigan, and then to Green Bay, Wisconsin where he collected an entire boat load of furs. His boat, The Griffin, was sent home with instructions to return and pick up LaSalle and his associates. The Griffin never returned, having been lost at sea. LaSalle decided to return home overland from his location on the St. Joseph River in southwest Michigan and thus became the first European to traverse the Michigan peninsula as he trudged on foot across the state to Detroit.

A Woodcut of Le Griffon, First Sailing Vessel on Lakes Michigan & Huron

The Sault became the first permanent place for fur trading. Priests Charles Raymbault and Isaac Jogues came to the Sault in 1641, and began the first temporary mission in Michigan, which was permanently established by Father Marquette in 1669. A party of Jesuits arriving in March of that year is reported as having found there twenty-five French traders who claimed that a most profitable commerce had sprung up. Soon, the traders discovered that many Indians preferred to trade at their summer camp 50 miles to the south at a place they called Michilimackinac. The trade became so popular there that by 1689, Sault Ste. Marie was practically abandoned as a trading post and from then on formed merely a station on the trade route to the Northwest, and was not re-established until 1750. Instead, Mackinaw became the favored site for the trade. No records are available that show Roscommon was visited by Frenchmen during this period for trade. It is unlikely since most of the trade took place at the major trading sites and Indians traveled to these places with their furs.

As the new century dawned in 1700, an ambitious young man in Montreal who took on an imperious-sounding name, Antoine de la Mothe Cadillac, and pretending to be of noble birth, convinced his superiors that the straits at the bottom of Lake Huron would make an ideal site for a new trading post. He turned out to be correct. At his urging, Indians from all around the Great Lakes moved to be near the little trade center he called Detroit. Almost immediately, it took the lead in peltry traffic and the former trading centers at the Sault Ste. Marie, Michilimackinac, and along the St. Joseph ended or dwindled to insignificance. Detroit became Michigan's only depot of trade during the early years of its existence. Roscommon furs would have traveled to the south during this period.

The Detroit post was not without problems. After a number of years the problems became more and more onerous and the independent traders began to trade again at other areas. Some returned to trade once again at Michilimackinac, while others established posts at The Grand and St. Joseph and Kalamazoo Rivers. The French authority over the trade ended with the fall of Quebec in 1759 as the French and Indian war came to a close. No longer were trade goods coming only from French-approved suppliers, on French vessels through French ports. Suddenly, the higher quality, lower cost English goods were available through the traders who paddled west from Montreal. Many of the men who did the paddling and stood behind the rude counters at the trading centers continued to be French or half-breeds, but their masters were now those who spoke English instead of French and were less likely to live among the Indians than the French traders.

England steered the fur trade in North America for the balance of the 18th century and into the 19th century until the upstart Americans demanded their just deserts after winning the War of 1812. Once again, the masters of the trade changed and an energetic American named John Jacob Astor became dominant from his headquarters on Michilimackinac. The Indians in the remote areas were unaffected by this change as the local traders continued to be French or half-breeds, or independents who paddled into the remote areas with their canoes laden with goods.

It is certain that Roscommon Indians received trade goods inasmuch as at least one artifact has been found that would have been carried by a voyageur. The Indians at Roscommon probably sensed little difference in the trade when the masters of the trade changed from the French to the British and finally to the Americans. They had to carry the furs they harvested in Roscommon streams and forests to the nearest trader just as before, receive their goods in the fall and promise to return in the spring with furs for payment .The furs still provided them with goods, liquor, and trinkets, but they obtained more and better quality goods from the English than the French. After the Americans became ascendant, the trading system changed somewhat as the American John Jacob Aster worked relentlessly to monopolize the trade.

Metis Voyageurs
HBC c.1821

Wikipedia Art

Metis (half –breed French and Indian) voyageurs are ready to load a bundle of furs in front of a trader's cabin. The trader (man with hat in rear of picture is directing work.) The bundles are standard size packs, each weighed 90 pounds.

Astor had important contacts with the government and he made certain that laws passed regulating the trade were to his benefit. The American system of trade provided for *factories*, a trading house under the supervision of government officials to keep the Indians supplied with goods and protect them from greedy traders intent on cheating the tribes with whiskey as the bargaining tool. Astor used the factory system to his advantage and worked to drive out competing traders. He sent his traders into the wilderness at large Indian gathering areas and he tried to prevent the remaining independent traders from gaining a foothold into the business. Ultimately he succeeded and his company became the major force in the fur business.

No fur trading outposts were located in Roscommon or surrounding counties. Instead, the nearest posts under Astor's control were located predominantly along the coasts at the mouths of the major river systems. Trading posts nearest Roscommon County were located at Grand Traverse, at the mouth of both the Au Sable and the Manistee and downsteam at the forks of the Tittabawassee near present day Owasso.

The trading posts along Lake Michigan from Grand Traverse to the Grand River were controlled by Rix Robinson. Robinson was employed by Astor after Astor had purchased several earlier posts operated by Madame La Framboise. Robinson successfully took over the La Framboise trading posts and operated them for a number of years.

Madam La Framboise was an unusual trader, a woman in a rough business dominated by ruthless men who knew how to bargain and were undeterred in dealing with Indians who were often difficult. How she came to be a trader is worth repeating. Her husband was Joseph La Framboise, a Frenchman who had become a successful trader in part, because he married his Madame, an Ottawa squaw, and thus earned the trust of the Ottawas that he dealt with. He conducted his trading among the Indians who lived along the Grand River near present day Grand Haven in Ottaway County. La Framboise spent his summers in Michilimackinaw assembling his outfit and traveled each fall to the Grand River with two boats loaded with trade goods. In the fall of 1806 while he and his wife Madelaine were paddling to his post he met with a group of Indians at the mouth of the Muskegon River who indicated they wanted to trade.

Joseph signaled his voyageurs to make for the shore and the party began unloading gear for an overnight camp. Joseph followed his normal practice of furnishing each Indian a drink of whiskey before the bargaining began. After the preliminary drink, one Indian named Nequat demanded more whiskey. Joseph refused. The Indian stomped away in a rage. Sometime later he returned while Joseph was kneeling in prayer. Without hesitation or warning he pointed a firearm at Joseph and fired. Joseph slumped to the ground dead.

The 26 year old Madelaine ordered the voyageurs to load the lifeless La Framboise into the boat and the party proceeded south toward the Grand River that had been Madelaine's home before she was married. There, she buried her husband and then made a momentous decision. She decided to continue in the trade without her husband. She gave orders and the party continued upriver to their post near present day Grand Haven where Madelaine took charge and began a life as a female trader in a rough business dominated by men.

 Once there, she began dealing with the tribesmen, insisting on fair and honest trades with all the Indians who came to barter. The Indians were impressed with a female who could speak with men on their terms and was not cowed by anyone. During her first winter in the woods a group of Indians appeared at her post with the murderer Nequat in tow and demanded that Madelaine decide his fate, assuming that she would employ the native remedy of an eye for an eye. She is reported to have told them, "I will forgive him and leave him to the Great Spirit." The natives grudgingly obliged, although some time later he was found dead with a knife in his heart.

 Her first year alone was a success and she returned to Mackinaw loaded with just as many furs as she and Joseph had in prior years. She capitalized on her results by hiring men to open other posts under her supervision. Soon she was one of the most successful traders in Michigan earning five to ten times the amount earned by other traders.

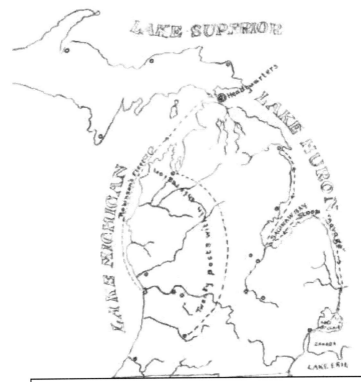

Dots show the location of trading posts owned by Astor
(from the 1919 book The Michigan Fur Trade by Johnson)

After the War of 1812 the American government required that the fur trade should reside exclusively in the hands of American citizens. John Astor had long been envious of Madame's operation and he finally succeeded in getting her to serve as an agent for the American Fur Company. In 1821, the long serving Madame finally retired to Mackinaw Island where she became a respected citizen and philanthropist providing aid to Indian boys and girls. Astor replaced Madame with his most respected trader, Rix Robinson, who supervised more than a dozen posts from the Grand River up to Grand Traverse.

Madelaine's daughter Josephine married the commandant of the fort, Captain Benjamin Pierce. (Pierce was the brother of Franklin Pierce who became President of the United States). The wedding was the largest event ever held on the island with all the military men dressed in their officer's uniforms resplendent with gold braids and ladies in their finest satin dresses. Madelaine surprised the leading citizens of Mackinaw by dressing in her native garb, a deerskin adorned with beads and porcupine quills.

A Painting of Madelaine displayed at The Harbor View Inn on Mackinaw Island

There weren't any trading posts or established traders in Roscommon; therefore, Roscommon Indians traded their furs with a trader on one of the rivers that flowed from their homeland, the Tittabawassee, the Au Sable or either of the west flowing rivers, Manistee or Muskegon. There was a trader waiting for them downstream at each location.

The trading post that may have been easiest to reach was the one on the Tittabawassee. A post had been established there by two brothers named

Williams. The brothers had established good relations with Indians along the river and were successful and ambitious. The brothers soon established another post along the mouth of the Au Sable River and provided trade goods to that outpost via a sloop that sailed along the coast. The boat, *The Savage,* regularly plied the waters between The Au Sable and Detroit, carrying peltry and trade goods.

A succession of traders operated at the mouth of The Au Sable for many years. The first trader at the Au Sable may have been George Shead who was followed by another trader named John V. Riley who married a prominent Chippewa squaw, Menaucumegoqua. The pair had several children, John, Peter and James, all of whom were given substantial land allotments in an American effort to obtain the land of the Chippewa in 1819. By 1823, the French trader Louis Chevalier ran the post at the mouth of the Au Sable.

The first white man to visit Roscommon was likely a traveling fur trader or trapper in the late 18th or early 19th century traveling via the Au Sable/Manistee Rivers. None left a written record of their visit. Since the Indian population in Roscommon was likely small, no traders would have established a permanent post and Astor's American Fur Co. records do not show any traders assigned there. The first written report of a white man traveling to Roscommon comes to us from Benjamin Williams, a member of the Williams family of fur traders. His story is recounted in the following chapter.

Chapter 5

Birthing of a County

The birthing of Roscommon required an unusually long gestation period; some 87 years from conception to birth before the State marked off its present border and sanctified its name as Roscommon. Other counties in other states were set off, named, and put in operation much sooner. Roscommon, like its nearest neighbors, was content to remain in the background as an isolated wilderness, home to a few indigenous people, several lakes and streams, and millions and millions of trees.

Most everyone would agree that the conception of Roscommon lay in that remarkably forward-looking document, The Northwest Ordinance of 1787. This law was adopted by the Congress of the young United States of America ostensibly to set out requirements for the formation of states from the Northwest Territory, - but it did much more. First, and perhaps most importantly, it gave credence to the idea that somehow, lands to the west of the first 13 states were destined to become part and parcel of the United States; some years later that idea was referred to as Manifest Destiny. The Ordinance also established that local units of government be defined by a new survey system that established regular land boundaries, our present system in use throughout the country west of the Alleghenies. Under the Northwest Ordinance, counties were set up with equally-sized townships on which local governments could be based. The system worked well then and now and replaced the old survey system of metes and bounds that had given rise to numerous problems of confusing and overlapping boundaries.

Before the Northwest Ordinance, the lands to the west were up for grabs. Ambitious land speculators, (including George Washington and Benjamin Franklin) were interested in obtaining title to some of these lands for personal gain along with several of the existing states and state governors. The Northwest Ordinance thwarted some of those potentially damaging ambitions and set out a careful procedure for the new lands to become independent states of the new republic, this, despite the fact that the lands were already claimed by England and inhabited by Indians who **knew** the lands belonged to them as a gift from the Great Spirit. Nevertheless, the Ordinance helped in making most Americans feel compelled to occupy and control the lands bounded by the Great Lakes.

The question of who owned the Northwest Territory was settled by the War of 1812. It was a war between England and The United States in the east, but in the Northwest Territory it was a war between the United States and a confederation of Indians and English troops. When the Americans won the war, the Indian confederation under the warrior Tecumseh collapsed. Thereafter, Indian resistance to the invasion of whites in the Michigan territory was essentially ended.

The end of the war allowed the successful Americans to negotiate treaties with the tribes for the lands they so earnestly desired. The first of the major treaties was personally negotiated by Territorial Governor Lewis Cass. Cass arranged the treaty discussion using some of his own funds since the government had failed to live up to earlier commitments and owed money to the tribes. His was The Saginaw Treaty of 1819 signed at the remote outpost of Saginaw. The terms of this treaty required the Chippewa to give six million acres of Michigan land to the U. S. government – most of the eastern half of the state. Roscommon Indians must have felt the tide turning against them when these events were learned. The lands along the Au Sable River were suddenly owned by Americans who lived in the south around Detroit. The natives around Roscommon wondered how those people could be so greedy since it seemed there were so few of them for so much land.

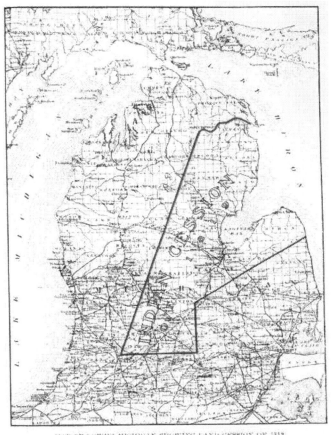

MAP OF LOWER MICHIGAN SHOWING LAND CESSION OF 1819

The Inset Area was Ceded by The Saginaw Treaty

In two more years the Treaty of Chicago was signed and a mixed group of several tribes signed away land rights to southwest Lower Michigan. More was yet to come for the Roscommon Indians.

The reminder of all Indian lands in the Lower Peninsula and half the Upper became the property of the Americans with the signing of the Treaty of Washington in 1836. The land given by this treaty was the western part of the Lower Peninsula (including Roscommon) and the eastern half of the Upper Peninsula. This treaty was negotiated at the direction of Lewis Cass and the War Department by Henry Schoolcraft, one of Cass's most trusted officials. This document was signed in Washington, D. C. by the ranking Chiefs of the Ottawa tribe. The treaty listed Mikenok [Mikenauk] twice, first by name as an Ottawa "Chief of the first class" living at "Grand Travers" entitled to a $500 one-time payment from the government. The second time the treaty listed his name he was recorded as a Chief among the Ottawa living along the Carp River.

The Lands Ceded by The Treaty of Washington 1836 (S. E. Michigan was ceded by the earlier Treaty of Detroit 1807)

Little else is known of Mikenauk or Mikenok. He is believed to have converted to the Christian faith sometime before 1843 since he is listed in the records of The Mission Church (organized 3 Jun 1843) in the present town of Old Mission, Grand Traverse County. When the Indians moved across Grand Traverse Bay to Leelanau County, Rev. Dougherty moved the Mission Church to the present town of Omena.

Even before the 1836 treaty had been signed, the energetic and impatient American officials began assessing how to open the vast wilderness for travel and settlement by whites. What was needed were roads and the wilderness area of Roscommon had none except for a few Indians paths that were useless for travel by pack animals or wagons, or anything beyond a man with a rifle and a small bag for travel necessities. Indian paths were so narrow that they permitted only a single file line of men willing to undergo exposure to mud, fallen trees, wash-outs, swamps and a lack of signs pointing the way to anything. (Actually, Indian paths were marked with signs. The signs were so subtle that even American woodsmen had trouble seeing and reading them. A typical Indian sign of a tree trunk bent in an unusual, unnatural fashion was a road marker for observant tribesmen. One such marker was noted near Roscommon along the Saginaw Trail).

The first American effort to open the vast territory north from Saginaw led to the first recorded visit to Roscommon by a white person. In 1835 the government commissioned a survey team to find a route through the interior to Mackinaw so that a road could be created. The task was assigned to the U.S Army's Topographical Engineers commanded by Lt. Benjamin Poole. Lt. Poole started from the village of Saginaw and moved north following the Tittabawassee River. After a month of hard work, the command had only made 20 miles through the forest and Lt. Poole was ill from malaria. The party reached the Williams Brothers fur trading outpost at the forks of the Tittabawassee where Ephraim and George Williams traded. Another William's brother, Benjamin, happened to be visiting when Poole and his men arrived. Poole was impressed with Benjamin and hired him to take over leadership of the surveying party for the road.

Benjamin conferred with his brothers and agreed to take on the work. He first reorganized the party and hired local men to assist including an Indian, Young Bear, to act as guide and interpreter. The hiring of an Indian for the work was an excellent idea as there were numerous Indian trails throughout the area and Indian travel to Mackinac using the trails was common. The problem was that the trials were only a foot or two wide and difficult to follow.

Benjamin began the undertaking by taking a single man and hiking due north until the two reached the headwaters of a powerful stream that he felt certain must be the Au Sable. The mouth of the river was well known by the Williams Brothers since they had visited there numerous times in consequence of their fur trade. Benjamin decided that the path he and his hired man had taken to the headwaters of the Au Sable would be suitable for a road. The two men returned to the forks and assembled the survey party along with their tools including a team of horses. The group began working their way north, avoiding swamps and streams and cutting trees and brush to make a six-foot wide road. After proceeding about 30 miles they came to the Au Sable again and Williams decided that additional supplies would be needed for the party to continue their work to the north. The pack animals they had brought, a team of horses, were completely spent and unable to return down the road they had just cut. Accordingly, Benjamin decided to send one man all the way back to Saginaw to obtain additional supplies. He was directed to load the supplies in one or more canoes, hire whatever Indians he needed, and proceed along the coast and then paddle up the Au Sable to meet with the road-building party.

Williams and the road builders continued their work for several days working their way to the north. After 16 days their provisions were nearly gone and the supply party had still not met up with them. Williams directed a forced march back to the Au Sable in search of the re-supply group he had commissioned. No one was at the headwaters and so the party waited. After three days their food supply was nearly gone. Williams and Lt. Poole decided to build a boat and go down the Au Sable in search of the supply party while the others waited. They made a crude dugout and, along with two other men, put their boat in the water for a downriver trip. The first day they paddled in silence all day without hearing any sign of the rescuers. At the end of the second day, their progress downriver was stopped by a huge dam of deadwood that had fallen and plugged the stream. The four exhausted men decided to stop for the night. Unbeknownst to them, the rescue party was camped just one bend downriver from them. The next morning, someone in the rescue group fired a rifle and the sound reverberated to the Williams group who made a rapid dash to the supply boat and their first good meal in days.

The explorers had significantly underestimated the difficulty in ascending the Au Sable. The supply party had spent days climbing over deadfall, negotiating shallow, swampy areas and having a hard time with the swift current in some areas. They had made numerous portages around various obstacles and finally met the downriver Williams boat after 13 days of hard paddling.

Williams and the supply party quickly made the trip upriver to the rest of the work group at the headwaters. The men there had consumed all their remaining food and were overjoyed at seeing Williams and Poole return. After eating and resting, most of the entourage returned home, leaving Roscommon to its isolation one last time. Williams, Poole and a few others continued the trek north following the headwaters of the Au Sable. After a trying journey where the entourage was reduced to eating berries for sustenance, they finally came to the shores of a large lake later determined to be Mullet Lake. They traced the edge of the lake looking for signs of habitation and rescue. One of the men spotted a single moccasin print in the muddy shore. They followed the direction of the print until they found others that led them to an Indian village. The Indians in the village were astonished to see them and hear them speak the Chippewa tongue.

The Indians fed the ragged party of men and, after they had rested, escorted them to the Cheboygan River that they followed till they arrived at Lake Huron. From there they made the short trip to Mackinaw and a measure of civilization. The group recovered for several days and then boarded a schooner for transportation to Detroit. The following year, Lt.

Poole returned to Mackinaw and repeated the trip in reverse, making surveying observations for the road to the Au Sable, thus establishing a complete route through northern Michigan.

Poole and Williams didn't record any particular observations pertaining to the Roscommon area but their road and the fact of their journey was the first step in the discovery of an area that had been previously absent of white travel. No one planted a flag, no one gave a speech, but the area was somehow different; now white settlement could begin in earnest.

The year of 1835 was a pivotal year for the Williams Brothers and for Michigan's North Country. In the same year that Poole and Williams completed their journey through Roscommon, the Williams' Brothers also built and operated the first steam saw mill in the Saginaw valley. They sawed lumber and sold it locally for the first settlers in building homes and barns. Less than 20 years later, their success at the mill was followed by others; 29 saw mills were built on the Saginaw River that were cutting 100 million board feet of lumber each year. An economic fire of gigantic proportions for the entire North Country of Michigan had been ignited.

By 1837, all the requirements set out by the Northwest Ordinance had been satisfied and Michigan was ready to become a state. The Territorial Governor, Lewis Cass, shepherded the paperwork through Congress and the new State of Michigan was born. Cass went about setting up the machinery of the new state and hiring people to help. Two of the most noted persons that he assigned to positions of authority were Henry Schoolcraft and Douglas Houghton, the first State Geologist. Schoolcraft was the Indian Agent at the Sault and he had already assisted Cass in negotiating the 1836 treaty. Now Cass asked Schoolcraft's help in naming the counties, the next layer of government. Schoolcraft, married to a Chippewa woman and an expert in Indian affairs, chose appropriate county names based on the Indian tribesmen who lived in the various localities. Thus, the Roscommon area became Mikenauk and it was administratively attached to Mackinaw County.

Douglass Houghton   **Lewis Cass**

Cass was much impressed with the young man Dr. Douglass Houghton and he gave Houghton the assignment of investigating the new land for its mineral content, especially since the presence of copper had long been hinted at by Indians from the north. The assignment to Houghton was reinforced by Cass's successor, the Boy Governor of Michigan, Stevens T. Mason.

Douglass Houghton was a successful doctor in Detroit, a large landowner, and an eminent scientist. He was also best friends with Stevens T. Mason, the first governor of Michigan in 1837. Mason was concerned that Michigan was getting bad press with westward immigrants as an unhealthy, cold and poor farming state, and so he worked with Houghton to commence a complete state survey, including geology, botany, zoology and topography aspects. Houghton assembled a crack team, including Bela Hubbard (assistant geologist), Sylvester Higgins (topographer and map maker) and Columbus Douglass (assistant geologist). The team systematically moved from county to county, recording vast amounts of information for processing into maps and written reports. Houghton issued a report in 1841 and noted the copper deposits and made a cautious statement concerning the possible iron ore in Marquette.

Houghton's brilliance was cut short in 1844 while he was investigating copper deposits in the Upper Peninsula and a storm came up on Lake Superior. Houghton's boat capsized and the young man drowned in the icy cold water. His corpse was recovered several months later on the shore of Lake Superior.

The U. S. General Survey Office had begun surveying the state in 1815. They first established a baseline (the main east - west line across the lower peninsula) and a meridian line (the north - south line intersecting the center of the lower peninsula). By the late 1830's, the Survey Office was ready to survey Roscommon County. The surveyor who was awarded the contract for all the sections in Roscommon was one John Brink, an Irishman who had suitable credentials for surveying work.

Brink won the contract for Roscommon in late 1836 and set out to hire helpers and begin actual work on March 1, 1837. (Surveyors often worked during the winter months so they could cross frozen swamps, rivers, and lakes and make accurate readings with their compasses and chains.) Brink and his crew established section lines throughout the county including areas around the largest lake in the state (Houghton Lake). Brink penciled in a name for the lake, *Muskego,* presumably because the water drained into the Muskegon River. (Other names given for the big lake for short periods were Red Lake and Roscommon Lake. None of the names stuck until the State of Michigan Legislature mandated the name Houghton Lake in 1879 to honor the young geologist who contributed much to the state in its earliest days.)

By 1840 the Roscommon survey work was completed and the county was completely established and all the sections defined in accordance with the survey system established with the Northwest Ordinance, a perfect square, 24 miles by 24 miles, with the townships listed as 21 through 24 from south to north and the ranges listed as 1 through 4 from east to west. Roscommon Station was thus situated in Town 24, Range 3.

Brink's survey maps were approved by his superiors at The Bureau of Land Management and they are no doubt accurate renderings of the

Roscommon area. The maps, however; seem to be lifeless documents as they show land forms, lakes and streams with no names and no comments except for the Musklego Lake as noted. Neither the South Branch of the Au Sable nor Robinson Creek was given a name, for example.

William Burt was given a survey contract in 1850 and 1852 to re-survey some of Roscommon. His work in and around the present village of Roscommon included establishing a witness tree along the South Branch River just north of Michigan Highway 18. The witness tree still stands and can be identified by a plaque that has been placed there. In comparison to Brink's map, that shown by Burt is more descriptive. He shows and names the Au Sable River, indicates a burnt area along the stream we now know as Robinson Creek and indicates a beaver pond on that stream as well. Burt further indicates that he found an Indian lodge and an Indian canoe adjacent to the beaver pond.*

Surveyors were required to provide Field Notes in addition to the maps they drew and the compass locations of each survey marker or witness mark that they placed at the corners of each surveyed section. Brink had penciled in the name Forginson Lake for the water we now know as Higgins Lake. Indians had lived around the area as evidence of their presence was noted along the shores. They trapped and hunted in the area and called the lake "Majinabeesh" (Sparkling Water). In his re-survey around Higgins Lake, Burt noted the presence of an Indian encampment on the south shore.

*[Author's Note - It has been reported that the village of Roscommon was located on the site of an earlier village named Robinson. According to a published account, this village was reportedly founded by a fur trader before 1845 named Geo. C. Robinson. No corroboration of this could be found in the available literature. Further, if such a site existed it would be expected to have been noted by the original surveyors of the county or other visitors or the railroad when they first laid tracks to Roscommon Station and such was not the case.]

Here are two of the Field Notes from the area around Lake St. Helen by Brink and then later, Burt.

<u>Town 23 Range 1, Section 1 –</u>

"This line passes over a level country not much better than swamp [with] 3rd rate hemlock, birch, maple, pine, cedar, tamarack and spruce. The water in the lake is red color –looks something like brandy. **April 21, 1839, John Brink"**

"General Description – the surface of this township is gently rolling, sandy soil, timber is yellow pine, white pine, aspen, birch, white and black oak, hemlock, etc. In the swamp there is cedar, tamarack, ash, spruce, fir, aspen, pine and alder.

Nearly all the east ½ of this township is sandy pine openings and plains. Most of the southeast quarter is level, 3rd rate land, wet, heavy soil. Sections 16 through 21 and 29 and 30 have good yellow and white pine timber for lumber. The lake in this township (Lake St. Helen) is shallow and muddy. The pond and stream (Au Sable River) in sections 9 & 16 is an arm of the lake, partially grown over and abounds in wild ducks and fish. **26th of August, 1852, Wm. Burt"**

Note that neither Brink nor Burt identified Lake St. Helen by any name and neither man mentioned seeing any Indians or Indian villages on the north shore of the lake. The Indian evidence was well-hidden Archaeological excavations after 1988 demonstrated that Indians had lived at this site for many years.

While Brink was surveying Roscommon, Sylvester Higgins was drawing section lines in various areas of the Upper Peninsula. After he left his post with the Geological Survey, his reputation suffered a serious blow; other surveyors in 1849 discovered glaring mistakes in his work, suggesting that Higgins had taken a number of short-cuts and avoided some of the real work.

Other surveyors were hired to repeat the work that Higgins had done. William Burt apparently was not too concerned about Higgins' fall from grace; his 1852 survey map of the big lake in Town 24 ranges 3 and 4 listed Higgins' name on the lake in Burt's beautiful flowing script. It has remained Higgins Lake ever since.

Curiously, Burt's map of Higgins Lake area had a railroad running adjacent to it along the Indian path known as the Saginaw trail. This map was made in 1852, 20 years in advance of the railroad line that was actually located several miles to the west.

The County's name Mikenauk didn't last very long after it was assigned by Schoolcraft. In 1843, a state representative, Charley O'Malley, had some county names changed from Indian monikers to Irish names such as Clare, Antrim and Roscommon. O'Malley happened to be from Roscommon, Ireland and he felt compelled to honor the Irish heritage of Michigan since the Irish were well represented in the state including many of the lumberjacks that were beginning to work in the forests (Ros, a wooded promontory or pleasant place while Coman was the name of an Irish saint who lived between 550 and 550 AD). The Michigan legislature didn't object to O'Malley's proposal and the legislative report was terse, *"The name of the County Mikenauk , as now recognized by law, is hereby changed to Roscommon,"* March 8,1843.

First Capitol of Michigan Built in 1828 in Detroit where the important decisions affecting the organization of Roscommon were made

So, now there was a recognized county with its borders and township's sections carefully surveyed. It was open and ready for business according to the U. S. Government and the State of Michigan. Unfortunately, unless you were an Indian, a surveyor, or an outdoorsman used to spending days or weeks on the trail, the area of Roscommon remained an unreachable, mysterious wilderness. Only a few surveyors, traders and adventurers had even seen the remote area and no one had any records to show the natural resources of the county other than the few notes from the surveyor's records.

The surveyors Brink and Burt and their assorted helpers were required by contract to produce maps, locations of the witness markers they left behind, and field notes of the lands they traversed as they completed their survey work. The U. S. General Survey Office contracts for survey work did not require that the surveyors remain silent about what they had witnessed and so, word slowly circulated about the wonderful stands of big pines that the men found in Roscommon and other areas in north-central Michigan. Roscommon lands were about to be discovered.

As rumors began floating about the potential riches in northern Michigan, a few men with foresight decided to investigate the area. They hired land-lookers, those sturdy outdoorsmen who could read and interpret survey maps, to visit the remote areas. Interest in the north was further stimulated by the U. S. Government who wanted to make the new lands available for settlement. In 1862 President Lincoln supported the Homestead Act, a law to provide free land in the newer, unsettled areas to those willing to homestead an area for at least five years. The Homestead Act helped many poor settlers, a large number of whom were immigrants, realize the American dream of independence and prosperity. This Act was an example of the opportunity in America for those willing to take risks and work hard in taming wild lands. The aim was to convert the wilderness to an agricultural landscape that would become a source of income for dedicated workers.

Many areas in northern Michigan presented a challenge to the requirements of The Homestead Act since the sandy soil and heavily forested regions made agriculture impossible. Some wags called the Act, *"a wager by the US government that they would bet you 160 acres of government land against five years of your life that you couldn't live on that land for five years without first starving to death."*

In spite of the hardships, The Act proved to be extremely popular and many Civil War veterans took advantage of free land from the government awarded to them for their service. Even with these inducements, it would be several more years before the lumbermen and the railroad arrived with enough people to bring a measure of civilization to the new county; one that was still covered with forests that had been growing for several hundred years.

Land-lookers & Railroads

The logging business in Michigan began in the Saginaw Valley alongside a number of streams, each of which provided power for a saw mill and a convenient method of delivery of logs to the mill. After the forests adjacent to the streams were each logged off, lumbermen began looking for new sources of logs for lumber. In order to find the sought-after timber, smart lumbermen turned to a professional for help: the land-looker, sometimes called a timber-cruiser. The men who practiced this profession were knowledgeable, hardy souls who could hike long distances and sustain themselves alone in the woods for prolonged periods.

Land-lookers needed to know the logging business. Their task was to act as an agent for a lumberman and furnish information sufficient to justify the outlay of large sums of money for purchasing land, establishing camps, and so forth. More specifically, the land-lookers searched for land with desirable timber that could be profitably logged, identified its precise location based on survey markers, and estimated the number of board feet in each stand of timber and then reported their findings without delay and without revealing the information to anyone else. The quality of a land-lookers' information could easily determine the success or failure of a logging venture.

Little has been written by and about land-lookers. The men who worked in the business were by necessity taciturn, generally bound by contract to keep all information secret so that the men who hired them, the lumber barons, could purchase land and begin logging before competition caused prices to rise. One of those who wrote of his experiences as a land-looker was David Ward, a man who ended up owning the largest pinery in Otsego County, one that required ten years to harvest all of the pine.

David Ward became known as a lumber baron but he got his start as a land-looker, identifying promising forest tracts for other lumbermen. In his autobiography, Ward notes that he was examining areas west of Saginaw and then in north-central Michigan in 1850. Ward said that both William Burt and John Mellen (another surveyor) told him about the big pines and he decided to concentrate efforts in the north central area. Ward examined a variety of tracts of land while he eworked under contract to several lumbermen. The news of his work gradually became known as word of land sales in northern Michigan began to spread about the lumbering community. Ultimately, Ward earned enough money to purchase land for himself and he began his own logging operations leading to his title as "King of Michigan Lumbermen."

One other source of news about the forests and lakes in Roscommon came from an unlikely source: The Detroit Free Press. In 1849 an outdoorsman of the first order named George H. Cannon decided to hike the state of Michigan from north to south. He started at Mackinaw and ended his long walk in Detroit where he promptly visited the Free Press to pass along the news. The Free Press dutifully reported his extraordinary walk on Oct. 6, 1849. Cannon had followed the Saginaw Trail and had camped at Higgins Lake. He was ecstatic about the lake and the nearby scenery. "This is the most beautiful of Michigan's 3,000 gems….Surrounded on all sides by elevated lands which are timbered with the spruce and yellow pine, with groves of aspen and oak, and containing a small island fringed with willows and densely timbered, it remains set by the hand of nature amidst wild forests of Michigan, a pleasant retreat among the hills."

News about Roscommon's forests and the big pine that gradually circulated among lumbermen was welcome news indeed. By 1840, lumbering was beginning to play out in the forests of Maine, New York and Pennsylvania and the lumber barons who operated in those areas were beginning to look for other regions. When Burt finished his re-survey of some Roscommon lands, Michigan was humming with the sound of saw mills operating in the coastal areas of Michigan, especially at Saginaw.

One of the Big Ones (*Nels Michelson Collection*)

Commercial lumbering started in the saw mill town of Saginaw and had rapidly spread to the river town of Muskegon on the west coast of the state as demand for lumber skyrocketed after 1850. From there, saw mills began sprouting ever further to the north on each major river system that could support a log drive. River-by-river, the loggers and the saw mills went north until they extended all the way along both the east and west coasts of the state. Especially large saw mill towns were developed on the west coast at Manistee and Grand Traverse as well as at Muskegon. The mills at these towns used Great Lake schooners as the means for transporting their lumber to Chicago where it was sold for use in Chicago or loaded on trains for further shipment to states in the great prairies that had little or no timber. The mills on the eastern coast of the state at the river towns of Saginaw, Au Gres, Au Sable and Cheboygan also used the Great Lakes for shipping to markets in the east and south.

All early logging operations were confined to areas within easy access of a river. The Saginaw drainage basin containing the Saginaw, Tittabawasse, Tobacco, Chippewa, Cass and Flint Rivers became a vast reservoir of timber for the infant logging industry. The tiny village of Saginaw with its fur trading post grew from a sleepy village of 400 people in 1836 to a thriving frontier town in 1855 with 23 saw mills along the Saginaw River. The town became a lumberjack's haven with taverns and bawdy houses lining the streets and competing with one another to satisfy the thirsty jacks and meet their basest desires. As the mills began shipping more and more lumber to Chicago and Albany, New York, the lumber barons grew wealthy and began looking for other Michigan regions to exploit. The value of Michigan lumber to the young, growing nation was hard to dispute. As immigrants moved westward, more and more lumber was needed especially in the Great Plains where not a single pine tree grew.

The very best pine in the world in both quality and quantity grew in north-central Michigan. The forests were large and they contained a variety of trees, hardwoods as well as conifers, all of which were valuable. White pine occurred in stands among other trees and it was those tracts the land-lookers searched for. The white pine was most sought after because of its size and light-weight, enabling transport at almost no cost via floating logs down the river. Many of the great white pines of Roscommon and neighboring counties reached heights of 125 to 170 feet tall with trunks from two to five feet in diameter. These giants were particularly sought after, not only because of their huge size, but also because most had few lower limbs making them knot-free and especially desired by wood-workers since the material could be easily shaped for a variety of purposes.

Another use of the knot-free pines was for the masts and spars of sailing vessels. The British with their huge sailing vessels especially favored the tall, straight pines for these applications and their appropriation of prime logs in the early days caused much consternation among the Americans.

As the message about the pines spread, investors began to make regular visits to the U.S. Land Office to enquire about buying Roscommon lands. The government had decided to sell the land for the low price of $1.25 per acre in order to stimulate development. Investors began buying Roscommon land in 1850, some 25 years before the county was formed. Examination of the Roscommon County Tract book shows the first purchasers of Roscommon lands were speculators and lumbermen. Buyers of smaller parcels of land, 160 or fewer acres, came mostly after 1870, and generally purchased land first in the southern tier of sections, moving north thereafter. One exception was George Robinson, a Detroit lawyer and land speculator, who purchased smaller tracts of land after 1870 all around the county. Robinson didn't seem to be particular about the kind of land he bought as his land purchases covered the gamut of farming lands, swamps, and forested land.

The U. S. Government gave away the largest share of Roscommon lands to the railroad to encourage a line to the remote area. The original plan was for the U. S. Government give away nearly half of the entire county: almost every other section of land was designated to be given to the railroad. In the end, this wasn't possible since some sections were purchased by land speculators before the railroad could get the alternate sections they wanted.

Roscommon County as originally defined by the Northwest Ordinance consisted then and now of 16 townships defined by the letter "T" for towns and "R" for ranges. The towns from south to north are towns 21 through 24 while the ranges from east to west are ranges 1 through range 4.(The numbering system is determined by the distance from the original survey baseline and meridian established for the state.)Thus the six mile by six mile square town or township in the southeast corner of the county is T21R1 (Town 21, Range 1) while the town in the northwest corner of the county is T24R4. A detailed study of the U.S Government tract book for the southern-most four towns, (Town 21, Range 1through 4) reveals that:

1. The U. S. Government gave the railroad an astonishing 29,650 acres of these Roscommon lands, some of it prime timber land. These gifts were given in 1861 and 1869 to the railroad that was later known as The Michigan Central upon their promise to build a line to and through Roscommon. This equates to nearly one third of the land in these townships.

2. The earliest purchaser of Roscommon land from the government was Eber B. Ward. Ward purchased Roscommon land in May of 1850 and on several dates in 1854 and 1855. He bought over 6,000 acres of land, virtually all of it listed as #1 and #2 pine lands. (A brief review of Ward's life, follows.)

3. Other large purchasers were Moore and Alger, 3,840 acres purchased in 1868, Geo. Frosh, 3,440 acres purchased at various dates in 1866, 1867 and 1868.

4. A female land speculator and the only one noted who bought Roscommon property, Emma Ripley, was one of the early land purchasers in 1868.

Large land purchasers for the second tier of sections to the north (Town 22, Range 1-4) were the following;

Emma Ripley, Moore & Alger, Geo. Frosh and Eber Ward, (all noted earlier) and Bundy & Loman, Alexander Swift and E. F. Gould each purchased several hundred acres of Roscommon land from the government. Gould had the distinction of purchasing a tract of land that was described as being exclusively #1 pine.

Town 23 lands:

Large buyers of these lands were Orrin T. Higgins, D. W. Bradley, R. A. Alger, Dodge & Phelps, John Belnak and the appropriately named John Woods. The well-known lumberman from Flint who was later to become the Governor of Michigan, Henry Crapo, also purchased a small tract in this area. Higgins was not one of the early buyers; he purchased his 1080 acres in 1874 some while after the earliest land speculators.

Town 24 lands:

The northern-most lands of Roscommon had fewer large scale land buyers who purchased land before 1870 compared to the more southern ranges. Buyers were David Rush, John Woods, D. A. Blodgett and David Peabody. One of the larger purchases was by Paullus Lux and James Cavanaugh. These men were from Lake City, Michigan and for some reason they bought a large tract of land that was listed in the Roscommon Tract Book as *"Swamp"*.

Another large land buyer was one who made a number of purchases all over the county over a period of several years, a Charles L. Ortman. Ortman began buying Roscommon land in 1872 and then he added more in 1875 and 1877 accumulating more than 3,000 acres. But the family wasn't finished; in 1885 and 1887 a Marie Ortman also bought Roscommon land. The Ortman's finished their buying spree with a final purchase in 1904 – they had purchased 3,890 acres of Roscommon land.

Most of the pine lands in Roscommon and other areas were purchased from the government and were in private hands by 1870, well before the arrival of settlers who were primarily interested in farming.

The first speculator in Roscommon land was Eber B. Ward (1811 – 1875), an interesting character with a story worth repeating. By the time he was purchasing Roscommon lands, he was already a millionaire in a time when salaries of a few hundred dollars per year were typical. He was easily the richest man in the Midwest, having earned a reputation (and a lot of money) with steamships

Ward began his working career as a cabin boy on vessel plying the Great Lakes. His industrious work habits caught the attention of his uncle, a shipbuilder from Saginaw, and prompted his hiring as a clerk in his ship-building business. Soon, Ward had learned the shipping business and had accumulated enough money to invest in a vessel of his own. He became a

Master of the vessel in 1835 and then partnered with his uncle in shipbuilding. They each became wealthy with the growth of trade from the port of Detroit.

Eber B. Ward

But Ward was nothing if not ambitious. He decided to branch out his investments and soon entered the lumber business which led to investments in railroads followed by further investments in steel-making in order to supply steel for the railroad industry. Ward seemed to have a Midas touch, as his steel company, The Eureka Iron and Steel Works, became the first in the U.S. to begin use of the revolutionary Bessemer process for making steel. Naturally, Ward began using this higher-quality steel to produce rail for the railroads at great profit.

Ward became president of the Pere Marquette Railroad Company, the firm that helped transport logs from mid-Michigan to saw mills located on the coast, including an important saw mill owned by, you guessed it, Mr. Eber

B. Ward. Ward's purchase of Roscommon lands was a part of his logging operations, although he died before logging in Roscommon reached the fever pitch that was to occur a few years after his passing.

During his life, Ward had become involved in many successful businesses. The result was that disposing of all his assets at his death was an extremely complex affair, made more so by the numerous heirs he left behind. Sadly, most of his direct heirs, his children, were found to be mentally incompetent. Ward's assets included iron, silver and copper mines, pine lands, saw mills, steel-making and rolling mills, silver smelting works, railroads, farming lands, and glass works. The services of several accountants were needed to manage and dispose of his estate after his death.

Eber B. Ward's Detroit Residence on Fort Street

Loggers and their lumber camps steadily crept north from Saginaw and The Tittabawassee River toward Roscommon as well as eastward from

Muskegon and Manistee. In 1867, the Danish lumberman Rasmus Hanson tramped eastward along the Manistee River. When he reached the headwaters of the Au Sable and Manistee Rivers and saw the great stands of white pine, he decided to go no further and set about the business of procuring timber lands. His partner was Nels Michelson (see Chapter 8) who built a home in Grayling but later became well-known in Roscommon when a village one mile west of Houghton Lake was named after him and his saw mill. By 1870 Roscommon was on the cusp of becoming an epicenter of logging along with its neighboring counties.

Roscommon became one of the largest suppliers of high quality white pine in the state. One lumberman alone, Henry Stephens, cut more than one billion board feet of lumber from Roscommon forests. Since logging became such a vital force in the settlement and economic life of early Roscommon, it is essential to understand the basic practice of logging in the late 19th century.

The universal measure of the quantity of lumber in a log was the number of board feet per log. A board foot was defined as a one inch thick board, 12 inches long and 12 inches wide. This measure was a theoretical estimate since the outer, round edges of the logs had no value and were scrapped generally by burning. Since saw mills cut lumber in a variety of sizes and thicknesses the number of board feet in a log was a theoretical measure of the value of a log. A 16 inch diameter log was generally presumed to contain 144 board feet. This means that loggers assumed the mills could obtain 12 boards that were 12 feet long in 16 inch diameter logs. Over time, it was shown that logger's estimates were surprisingly accurate.

Logging companies all employed a man who estimated the number of board feet in each log cut. His records were carefully kept and presented to the designated saw mills for payment. Generally, saw mills paid for logs when they were received at the mill although in many cases the loggers acted as a jobber for the mill in which case the mill provided advance payments to help assure the supply of logs.

The volume of lumber cut in Michigan continued to increase as the century wore on and the loggers came closer and closer to Roscommon and her treasure of green gold. In 1872 statistics for the output of saw mills around the state were as follows:

Location	Total Output (millions of board feet)
Saginaw valley	840
Muskegon	320
Huron Shore	180
Manistee	160
Grand Haven	150
Menonimee	140
Mills near Flint	110

As a point of reference, it is noted that the Grand Hotel on Mackinaw Island was built entirely of lumber during its erection in 1887. The massive building required 1.5 million board feet of lumber. The lumber for the hotel was harvested locally and sawed at a mill at St. Ignace by the hotel's builder, Charles Caskey. Caskey used predominantly white pine for the massive structure that he built with 300 men in three months' time.

Logging technology changed rapidly during the lumbering era in Roscommon. By 1873, commercial logging had come as come up the Tittabawassee as far north as Edenville, at the county line separating Midland and Gladwin Counties. The large logging camp here, Camp 16, was the source of many lumberjacks who later moved north to Roscommon County and its camps a few years later.

One of the early pioneers in the southern part of Roscommon was an early, small scale farmer and sometimes logger who cut and sold the pine from his own property. Albert Wickham and his family moved to Denton County, Section 20 and homesteaded 160 acres just a few miles distant from another early settler, Augustus Emory. Albert, a cattleman and butcher from Toledo bought his acreage with the intent of logging off the white pine and in the process earn from 50 cents to a dollar per log. He had decided to come to Houghton Lake for his wife's health. Mrs. Wickham had tuberculosis and doctors at the time recommended the north woods as the means to get clear, cool air which was believed to help in the cure of tuberculosis. The remedy apparently worked as Mrs. Wickham lived to be 101 years old.

Lumbering technology changed and evolved during the heyday of Michigan's lumbering period, 1840 – 1900, and also during the 25 years of Roscommon logging, 1875 – 1900. Before 1875 the loggers were entirely dependent on the weather as they needed cold to make ice roads in order to move logs from forest to the nearest waterway used for transporting logs to the saw mill.

Two events of especial importance to the lumbering business occurred during this period that had pronounced effect on the profitability of logging in the interior areas. The first was a development by a logger named Silas Overpack from Manistee. Silas operated like other loggers of his time – cutting trees only in the winter so he could use ice roads to move the cut logs. The universal practice was to use a team of horses to pull heavy sleds to the riverbank for the spring river drive. Lumberjacks felled trees with axes as near to the ice roads as possible before the sawyers cut off the branches and cut the logs to length. After that, the logs were rolled up a ramp made of stout limbs and onto the husky sled where they were carried to the river on the sled. It was an effective system that worked well – so long as the weather cooperated. A thaw during the winter prevented the use of the ice sled and effectively ended logging until the cold weather returned. In some years, warm weather had a huge negative affect on productivity that made the difference between profit and loss for many loggers.

In 1870, Silas began to tinker with the idea of using big wheels to tote logs in warm weather. After making several sets of wheels that were progressively larger and larger, he found that wheels with an eleven-foot diameter separated by a sturdy axle with a heavy chain attached at the bottom could easily carry three or four logs. Silas found that if he attached a long yoke or lever to the axle it became a simple matter to lift the logs by the attached chain and pull the logs wherever he wanted with a team of horses. Suddenly, summer logging became more practical.

Another major problem for loggers was the distance of the timber from the saw mills. River transport of logs had been the only means available since the beginning of logging but when difficulties were encountered in the long river drives considerable cost was added to the operation. Log jams on the river were common. One such jam on the Tittabawasse River was said to be 150 miles long. Jams of any sort added to the cost of logs, especially when dynamite or other extraordinary means were needed. What was needed was a low cost means for transporting logs from the forest to saw mill without waiting for the spring thaw. Railroads would work just fine if there were a way to get a railroad into the forest where the logs were. Almost as if ordered, Winfield Scott Gerrish solved that problem.

Gerrish was born to Mr.& Mrs. Nathaniel Gerrish of Maine, patriotic folks who named one of their sons after the most famous American General, Winfield Scott. Known as the "Grand Old Man of the Army," he served on active duty as a general longer than any other man in American history. Over the course of his forty-seven-year career, he commanded forces in the War of 1812, the Mexican-American War, the Black Hawk War, the Second Seminole War, and the American Civil War. He served as Commanding General of the United States Army for twenty years, longer than any other holder of the office. Scott was such a national hero that he was nominated for President.

Such was the namesake of the young Gerrish boy who grew up in the forests of Maine, watching his father as he worked in the Maine forests as a lumberman. In 1857 the family moved to Wisconsin. Young Gerrish was educated in the public schools and in 1865 as a 16 year old, was sent to the naval academy at Annapolis. He left the academy at the end of his first year, and returned to Michigan to enter upon an active business career as a lumberman.

He was 18 years old in the winter of 1867 and during that season he began operations as a lumberman on his own and took a contract to "put in logs" on the Muskegon. In the autumn of 1873, he made an extensive logging contract with a firm to put in a large amount of logs on a small creek. Unfortunately, that year was a dry year and the creek shrank to almost nothing. Gerrish began to build dams to solve the problem and was finally able to deliver the contracted logs. John L. Woods, a veteran developer of the lumber interests in northern Michigan, had heard the story of Gerrish's hard work in the dam building and offered Gerrish an interest in a tract of 12,000 acres owned by him on the upper waters of the Muskegon. In 1874 he added to this acreage a large tract of timber land in Clare Co., Mich., a location considered practically worthless for lumbering, as it lay remote from the river.

That was Gerrish's situation just before he took time off from his Muskegon logging business to attend the Philadelphia Centennial Exposition. While there, he saw an experimental, small railroad engine that was designed to run on a small gauge track. Gerrish returned to Michigan with the idea of using a small gauge railroad to help take his logs out of the woods. He bought a small Shay locomotive and built six miles of rail line straight into the woods where he was logging timber. The scheme worked. His railroad line soon became known across the state and lumbermen who owned remote timberlands all wanted their own railroad line. In little more than ten years there were more than 80 small gauge railroads operating in the woods thanks to Gerrish's development.

By January 1877, the Gerrish logging railroad was built a distance of six miles in the woods terminating at the Muskegon River. Within the following year the road was extended. During the first year it was operated, the "put" was 20,000,000 board feet; with the new facilities in 1879 the "put" reached a maximum of 114,000,000 board feet. In the spring of that year Gerrish & Woods bought an interest in the Hamilton mill at Muskegon, where the former fixed his residence in 1880. Mr. Gerrish, within that year, purchased a share of the Wilson mill at Muskegon and continued to hold a proprietary interest in several shingle-mills. In 1880 he made a purchase of the Saginaw Bay & Northwestern Logging Railroad, buying the route in company with W.J. Miller. During the next two years the firm transported

90,000,000 board feet of logs annually on its track.

In 1879 Gerrish passed the most active year of his business career. He banked and put into the Muskegon River 130,000,000 feet, and in the year following put in 100,000,000 feet. During these two years he was recognized as the champion individual logger of the world. The maximum number of men employed by him in his varied interests in 1880 was 4,000 in round numbers.

In 1882 Gerrish decided to use some of his wealth to build a new home. He commissioned construction of an elegant residence at Muskegon, at a projected cost of $30,000. He never was able to live in his new home as he took ill and died in 1882 at the home of his sister. He was 33 years old.

Gerrish Logging Train Passing Over a Temporary Trestle Bridge

Top Loaders Loading Logs for Transport

Practices in the beginning of logging in Roscommon followed earlier routines established in lumber camps all around the Saginaw Valley with separate jobs at the camps for specialized work. A most important job was the job of scaling the logs – the scaler. After the 'fellers' felled the logs, the limbs were removed by 'choppers', and the 'sawyers' cut the logs to length, the log scaler would measure the log's diameter, estimate the board feet and record the figures for a talley of the day's work. The scaler was a higher paying job, sometimes 2nd in pay and rank to the foreman or camp boss.

Scalers used standard assumptions for their calculations: 16 inch logs were assumed to contain 144 board feet, a 28 inch log 576 board feet, and a 36 inch log 1024 feet. A very large and occasionally encountered cork pine of 44 inches diameter would scale at 1600 feet. Roscommon was known to have lots of these giants. Scalers working in Roscommon forests routinely estimated logs at 1600 and sometimes 1800 board feet. In the early days of Roscommon logging, the lumbermen sought the cork pines and never cut anything less than 8- 10 inches with many loggers cutting logs no smaller than 16 inches in diameter. Their philosophy was to cut the best and leave.

Scaling Logs and Recording the Figures

The ice roads and the transport of logs was handled by teamsters that all lumbering camps employed. These men, some with their own teams of horses, were roused before the rest of the camp so they could hitch their teams and sprinkle water on the packed snow to create ice roads. All day long they would then use their teams to pull sleds over the roads carrying logs from the forests. The sleds were loaded and unloaded by other men in the camp called 'loaders.' The loaders carefully maneuvered thousand pound logs onto the sled and then chained the loads in place for delivery to the 'skid' where the logs were unloaded and piled awaiting the spring thaw and the high water.

The teamsters and loaders managed the transport of logs from the forest to the place where the logs were transported by rail or water. All these workers, often called shanty boys, needed support people: the filers to keep saws and axes sharp, a blacksmith to repair broken tools and chains, and a cook and cook's helper to feed the workers. The scaler and foreman managed the entire operation. Camps varied in size considerably depending upon the volume to lumber to be "put – in" during the logging season; some camps had no more than 30 shanty boys while others numbered more than one hundred.

Discipline in the camps was severe. Experience had taught the managers that the best way to avoid problems and the resultant work disruptions by the rowdy, testosterone-laden men was to remove all temptations. The men generally worked from daylight to darkness, ate their noon meal in the woods and had little time for tomfoolery of any sort. No alcohol or card-playing was allowed in camp and during meals in the camp kitchen, absolute silence was required. The hard rules worked and the men saved their fighting and drinking until Saturday night at the nearest town, saloon, and bawdy house. Wherever the lumber camps were located, a town was sure to follow. There weren't any towns in Roscommon in 1870 but the lumbermen from the south and west were eyeing the region and the lumber camps were soon to open.

The U. S. Government knew that northern Michigan could never prosper until railroads penetrated the area allowing people and goods to flow into and out of the area. But building a railroad through a trackless wilderness was an expensive proposition and no prudent railroad men were interested in investments of the size needed to open the north woods. The U. S. Government also didn't have the money or the political will to undertake the investment either, but they did have land – lots of it. And so the government decided to use a large part of the lands they wished to open as the means for generating the money to build the railroads. Negotiations were held with the nearest railroad, the Amboy, Lansing, and Traverse Bay Railroad Company. It was agreed that the government would reserve alternate sections of land to be given to the company in exchange for a new line.

Negotiations between the railroad and government were held before and during 1859. By 1860, just before the outbreak of the Civil War, the agreements were reached and land was signed over to the railroad company

RR construction crew - labeled" South of Bridge, Grayling
Post card on back dated 1910

Of course the railroad company wasn't interested in owning the land, they wished only for the income that the land represented and thus they soon established their own land sales to generate cash for building the line. The outbreak of the War Between the States halted most work and discussions about new construction. It wasn't until the war was nearly ended that serious efforts began for building a line north from Lansing to Owosso and then to Saginaw and Bay City. The company who took on the project was the successor to the Amboy, Lansing and Traverse Bay line, the Jackson, Lansing and Saginaw line who had purchased the old line and the rights to the land given by the government. A new series of negotiations and new grants of Roscommon lands were provided in 1869. (The railroad changed names one more time: The Jackson, Lansing and Saginaw line soon became known as Michigan Central in 1871.)

The railroad named a new Chief Engineer in 1869, a man named William Donovan. Donovan was told about the government land grants and the plan to extend their line all the way to Mackinaw. The President of the company asked Donovan to scout out the way north to determine if there was any reason a line couldn't be built as planned. Donovan solicited the help of two experienced outdoors men and the three began a long hike from Bay City on December 5, 1869. They followed the Saginaw Trail for 14 days of hiking, not encountering another human along the way. On the 15th day they reached the south shore of Higgins Lake in a blinding snowstorm. The men wisely pitched camp to wait out the storm. The next day the snow turned to rain and sleet and so the men waited another day. On the third day the snow and sleet was interrupted by brief periods when the wind blew so hard that the men could barely see the lake. They waited again. On the evening of the third day the wind broke. The men packed early on the fourth day and resumed their journey to Mackinaw, passing the length of the lake and continuing on the Indian trail until they reached civilization at Mackinaw. In spite of the hardships of the long hike, Donovan gave a positive report and the company decided to proceed in building the line north.

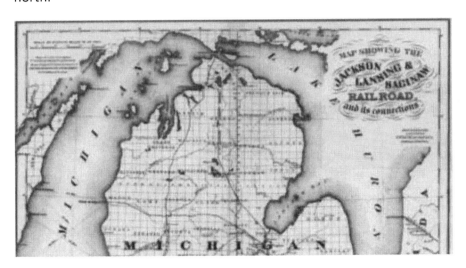

Early Map Showing the Jackson, Lansing & Saginaw Line to Roscommon

Finally, construction began and the line inched north from Bay City angling to the north through Standish and then northwest toward West Branch. Progress to the northwest was rapid: the company was said to have 600 men employed and they were able to sometimes lay five miles of track in one day. In May of 1872 the line reached St. Helens and then Roscommon Station and both stations were opened immediately by the railroad. The Chief Engineer, William Donovan, made regular trips to the two stations even as work continued in expanding the line to the north. For the first year of operation there was no way to turn the train around and so the train backed up all the way from Roscommon Station south to Bay City.

The following year progress in laying the track continued and the line passed through Grayling and then reached Gaylord with new stations being built along the way. The work stopped after the tracks reached Gaylord and final sections of tracks to Mackinaw weren't finished until 1881.

Roscommon, Crawford, and Otsego Counties were open for business and the hoped-for commerce in 1872. The railroad with its new station in Roscommon was like a magnet for lumbermen, settlers and tourists who had learned about the hunting and fishing in the region. Soon, tourists were venturing to the area and to other points further north.

The first station to the north of Roscommon Station was known as the Pere Cheney Station. George Cheney had gotten a land grant from the railway company to establish a stop on the railroad for fuel, freight, water and passengers. The location chosen was in Center Plains Township, Crawford County. Cheney built a saw mill, and later Cheney House to accommodate the growing number of settlers, lumbermen and tourists. On December 1st, 1874 Pere Cheney received a post office. By 1877 the village had another saw mill, a general store, a wagon maker, two carpenters, a doctor, a hotel telegraph service, and daily mail. In spite of its location in Crawford County, the Pere Cheney Station would soon play an important role in welcoming families to Roscommon's Higgins Lake.

One of the early visitors to Higgins Lake was an Indian who lived in Saginaw but ranged far and wide in the chase for game. His name was David Shoppenagon and he worked as a guide for wealthy Saginaw hunters. The Saginaw Daily Courier reported in 1873 that "Parties are now on their way to Higgins Lake who contemplate establishing a summer resort at that place...." One of the members of that party was Lorenzo Burrows, an employer of Shoppenagon as well as his friend. It was reported that Shoppenagon had guided Burrows to Higgins Lake and he was entranced by its beauty. The visit must have been a success as Burrows ultimately became a life-long camper at the lake along with his family and many friends.

By 1875 the camping at Higgins had become a family affair with wives and children from many of Burrow's friends in residence. The group spent several days camping with tents for each family group and a larger, main tent for food and cooking. The tents were arranged in a semi-circle among the green ferns nestled under the tall, stately pines with branches high above the campers. The camping lasted two weeks that first August in 1875 and Burrows followed up with arrangements to purchase 37 acres of land on the lake. The next year and every year thereafter, the two week campout stretched a bit until it became a summer-long event. The campers became regular customers at the small village of Roscommon as they arranged to purchase supplies and transportation to and from the lake to the railroad station.

The first road to Roscommon came as the brainchild of John Larkin, a businessman from Midland. Larkin decided that his business and that of the State could be improved if a road were made from Midland to Grand Traverse. He convinced the State Legislature of the wisdom of his proposal and the result was the building of a road that traversed Roscommon. After that, the State built the West Branch Road that ran along the south shore of Houghton Lake. At long last, travelers could reach the county with a degree of comfort.

The earliest lumbermen established the first winter lumber camps in the area and a handful of farmers began arriving from the south. These men and women were true pioneers; they came with teams of horses pulling all their belongings on wagons loaded with the tools necessary to start a life in the wilderness. The remote Roscommon County area was now on its way to becoming a busy, active place with lumbermen, vacationers and tourists and a few hardy farmers; each determined to take advantage of the riches in the wild, forested area.

Chapter 7

Lumbermen Arrive

Lumbermen began establishing camps in Roscommon County after the land-lookers scouted the land and the railroad established the means for delivering supplies. By the time camps were established, a few speculators had already purchased some choice parcels. Many of the lumbermen had directed their land-lookers to look for timber land along the river basins, the Au Sable, Muskegon and Tittabawassee, thus some of the early camps were located close to these rivers. The lumbermen who came for the pine varied widely; a few were principally small-time farmers who hoped to sell logs and clear ground to develop a farm while others were large, respected lumbermen of the type properly called lumber barons.

Henry Stephens (1823 – 1886) was by far the lumberman with the largest logging operations in Roscommon County. Stephens was a true lumber baron with an integrated operation that yielded profits in all phases of the lumber business from logging to lumber sales. His career spanned much of the logging era in Michigan as he began operations in southeast Michigan and moved north as the timber was exhausted in the lower part of the state. He retired before the lumbering era ended, giving his lumber business to his sons before his untimely death in 1888.

Henry Stephens' lumber business in Roscommon was largest of many because he was easily the largest land-holder, had the most men working in the woods, sawed the most lumber at his mill and cut the most logs in the county. He was a wealthy lumber baron before he came to Roscommon and he left even wealthier, turning the business over to his two sons, Henry (often called Tom) and Albert.

A Henry Stephens Mill at St. Helen

Another large Roscommon lumberman of the era was Nels Michelson. Michelson, like Stephens, started early in the lumber business in Crawford County but ended his lumbering career in Roscommon after much of the timber had been already logged off and most other lumbermen saw no further profit in the remaining wood left in the area. Michelson proved them wrong when he started a new mill on the west shore of Houghton Lake and ended up with an operation and a village named after him.

Henry Stephens was born in 1823 in Dublin, Ireland. His mother died when he was a young boy and in consequence, his father brought him to Ontario, Canada when the boy was but seven years old so that the two could live near Henry's aunt. Things weren't easy for the elder Stephens and he was forced to bind out his son to a farmer to make ends meet. After a stint of farm work, the boy then became a clerk in a country store and he and his dad managed to earn enough to support themselves plus a little extra that they carefully saved. When they had saved enough, the dad decided on a return visit to his beloved Ireland and the family remaining there. Sadly, the trip home was never completed as the ship and its passengers were lost at sea and Henry was never to see his father again.

Time passed and young Henry became an industrious lad, able to care for himself. When he came of age he decided that his prospects for success were better in The United States and so he made for the border and arrived in Romeo, Michigan with $300 in his pocket from his frugal living and hard work.

Relying on his experience in Ontario as a clerk, Stephens invested his money in a general store. The business soon became such a success that Stephens opened another store in nearby Almont, Michigan where he was one of the area's first businessmen. Things were going well for the young man who subsequently moved to Detroit with the idea of assisting his brother who had also ended up in Michigan. The pair suffered business problems during the panic of 1857 and Henry returned to Almont. Together with a man named John Wright, he expanded his operations with a hardware and lumber supply business. After the Civil War broke out in 1861, Henry received notoriety for two reasons: he was an ardent Abolitionist and he invested heavily in goods like cotton and nails that were in short supply due to the war.

As an Abolitionist, Henry became both a charter member of the new Republican Party and a supporter of runaway slaves. It became known in the small town of Almont that runaways could always count on Henry for help and his large home, particularly his basement, became a stop on the Underground Railroad.

Henry turned his wartime investments into a fortune and got heavily involved in the lumber business. His general store, like today's hardware stores, included a variety of goods needed for building with the all-important nails capturing center stage since the war effort had created a shortage for iron goods and especially nails. Henry saw no reason that he shouldn't capitalize on his large supply of nails and so he required that all would-be nail buyers purchase a corresponding allotment of his lumber. He was soon selling so much lumber that he needed a larger source of supply and so he purchased his own forest land with a good tract of timber eight miles northeast of Lapeer by Fish Lake. He then turned to three friends and raised $75,000 to purchase the land and build a lumber mill. Henry's fortune increased substantially with the profits from both his store and saw mill.

Since Fish Lake was not near any river, a branch of the Detroit & Bay City Railroad was built to it. By February, 1873, a village had grown up next to the mill with 26 private residences, a large hotel in process of construction, a store, a shoe shop, a livery stable, a blacksmith shop and a post office which was named Stephens. The saw mill manufactured large quantities of lumber, staves and shingles, but as with so many lumber towns, Stephens became a ghost town when the forest was consumed. Before the forests at Fish Lake were played out, Stephens looked elsewhere for logs and he found Roscommon with its much larger forests containing stands of large white pine. Henry, now a mature man with two grown sons, could hardly wait to get started in using his immense fortune to procure the green gold that he saw standing before him. Not only was there a fortune in pine just waiting to be cut, there was a railroad being built right to it.

By the late 1870's Henry Stephens knew as much about logging as anyone and he knew how to get things done efficiently. He started his operations in Roscommon by acquiring land and by purchasing an existing saw mill from another lumberman named Alex Swift. Stephens then established camps all around Lake St. Helen and launched two steam-powered barges to deliver supplies to the camps and pull rafts of logs to his saw mill for cutting. By 1880 Stephens had added another mill, this one a planning mill to allow manufacture of finished lumber. Of course, he also laid out a town complete with houses, office, a boarding house, schools and store.

An Early Albumen Photograph of St. Helen Forests

As the timber was depleted close to the lake, Stephens built a railroad into the forests to move the cut logs to the water. Unlike other loggers, Stephens cut everything, not wasting any timber because of size. His efficient mill managed to make a profit from logs as small as six inches in diameter. His was a large mill, capable of cutting 40 M board feet per year.

Stephens Logging Train Bringing Logs to the Mill
(Henry Stephens Logging)

Albumen Photograph of Another Stephens Mill

Stephens helped to make the Michigan Central Railroad a profitable operation. He avoided the higher cost of transporting logs by having his own saw mill at the source of the logs, yet he used the railroad to ship his finished product, the cut lumber. *The Roscommon News* in its usual brevity explained: "Dec 31, 1886 - "Some 500 car loads of lumber are shipped each month from St Helen."

Stephens was not one to be content. Even with his large operation at St. Helen he was on the look-out for other opportunities also. In the midst of his logging campaign at St. Helen, he found time to investigate another lumber operation at Bradford Lake near Waters, Michigan. The Roscommon News reported that on Nov 13, 1885 the Henry Stephens Co. bought out the firm of Wright & Davis of Bradford Lake. By then Stephens' two sons, Henry Jr. (often called Tom) and Albert were in the midst of taking over active operations of the company and by 1890 the signs were obvious – the timber around St. Helen was soon to be played out. In 1896 the huge firm closed their St. Helen operations and moved everything to Waters. It was reported that they had cut 1 billion board feet of lumber from Roscommon County. The village of St. Helen was nearly devastated by their move.

Henry Stephens Jr. was most commonly associated with the lumber operations in Waters. It was here that the younger Stephens built a farm and the famous bottle wall next to the road at his farm. His bottle wall (portions of it are still visible in Waters, Mi.) was an example of Tom's playfulness and generosity. Tom let it be known to all the children in the area that he was willing to pay cash money for any spent liquor bottles that the children brought to him. The word spread and in short order all the neighbor children were lining up with their found treasure that Tom happily purchased. Since there was no shortage of lumberjacks and mill workers in his employ, there were lots of empty beer and whiskey bottles all around the area.

The question of what to do with all the bottles was solved when Tom decided to construct a fence around his property and use the spent bottles in its construction. The fence became a landmark for the area and a playful reminder of the tastes of his workers. It was said that sometimes Tom would scatter large bags of empty bottles for the children to find whenever their pickings became slender and he would happily pay the children their bounty when they delivered the bottles.

The Bottle Wall (shown in Detroit News, Dec. 1946)

Henry Stephen's Barn: Said to be the Largest in Michigan

The lumbering business in the 1870's was a big business. Michigan ranked first in the supply of lumber for many years and in 1879, the logging business accounted for one in three Michigan manufacturing jobs – about 45,000 men. The business consisted of several parts: owning the forests, cutting the logs, transporting the logs and lumber, sawing and selling the lumber both wholesale and retail. There were profits to be made in each phase of the operation. Only a few men, like Stephens, were involved in all phases of the business. Others speculated in forest land or operated lumber camps or participated in the booming business, that is, the business of moving logs down the rivers to the nearest saw mill. Each of these businesses had financial risks but an upside potential of large profits.

The saw mill owners and operators generally bore the largest investment and had the opportunity for corresponding large profits if the market for lumber was robust. At the other end of the scale were jobbers, those who contracted with a saw mill to furnish a set number of board feet to be delivered to the mill in the spring at the conclusion of a winter's logging. Jobbers with ambition but no money could often finance the winter's work by advances from a mill, or by arranging credit to meet the needs of a logging camp and provide the monthly paychecks to the shanty boys.

Unlike Henry Stephens' route, most camps arrived in Roscommon as the lumbermen worked their way inland from the Great Lakes and up the major river systems. The saw mills at Muskegon provoked the creation of camps up the Muskegon River, those at Manistee caused the camps to move up the Manistee River toward Grayling and those at Oscoda and Au Sable provided the impetus for camps in Roscommon County within reach of the Au Sable after the coastal areas were depleted of their forests.

The saw mills and the lumber barons had a philosophy of logging that was based on greed and an expanding market that could make a man wealthy beyond his dreams: cut the most and the largest of the trees and then move on to other large tracts before someone else gets it. It was a philosophy of 'get rich quick' based on the implicit assumption that there would always be opportunities for the taking somewhere. The result of this philosophy was that the largest of the Roscommon forests were leveled quickly. Those lumbermen who remained often were able to make second and third cuttings of a forest as they used smaller and lower-profit trees for their operations.

106

Nels Michelson was an example of a self-made lumberman who became rich by logging the largest trees from first cuttings of forests at the direction of the mills. He then furthered his wealth by logging in Roscommon at the end logging era by focusing on lower-profit trees and trees for specific uses.

Nels was one of those early loggers to north central Michigan as he hiked along the Manistee River with his friend, partner and fellow Dane, Rasmus Hansen. The two were searching for pine lands upstream. They were jobbers, neither had enough money to own or operate a mill. As they came to the headwaters of the Manistee and looked over the pine in Crawford County, both men realized the profit potential by lumbering in this area. Consequently, they arranged financing to purchase land for themselves and then established contracts with Manistee mill owners promising to furnish logs to the mills' specifications. With hard work and prudent decisions, both men became successful lumbermen operating many camps around north central Michigan.

Nels Michelsen was born November 25, 1840, and attended the government schools of his native land until fifteen years of age, when he was bound out to a farmer for three years, receiving five dollars as compensation for his labors in the first year and ten dollars in the second year. He continued to work as a farm hand until 1864, when he joined the Danish army in the war with Prussia and was taken prisoner.

When the war was over and he was released, he returned home and again worked as a farm hand until 1866, when he came to the new world. Cholera broke out on ship and the passengers were held in quarantine at New York for two months during which time two hundred of the passengers died. By this time Nels had used up all his traveling money and was broke, nevertheless, he made his way to the home of his brothers in Racine, Wisconsin, and after remaining there for a short time went to Manistee, Michigan. He found work in a lumber camp for a dollar per day as a swamper and driver. As soon as he had earned enough to buy a team of horses he bid on, and won, a contract for hauling supplies to the lumber camp.

In Manistee he met some other young Danes, among them Rasmus Hanson. The two ambitious young men pooled their savings in 1869 of fifteen hundred dollars and bought the tools needed to begin a logging operation for a Manistee mill. The venture was short-lived; their bank in Manistee failed taking most of their funds. Both Michelson and Hansen started again as loggers and after a year the two men again organized a logging company, this time buying their own small tracts of pine land for logging. Meanwhile, the young Dane Michelson found a wife. In 1870 he married Margarethe Jensen and the two began a family, ultimately siring seven children. The oldest of the children was a girl, Karen Michelson.

Another Danish lumberman, Ernst Salling joined the partners and provided some financial assets and a new company emerged; The Salling, Hanson & Company of Grayling, Michigan along with another firm, The Michelson & Hanson Lumber Co. with Nels Michelson as President. The companies prospered, expanded and broadened their business base with each of the partners acting both separately and in partnership as circumstances warranted. Michelson, for example, became President of the Exchange Bank of Crawford County and served as a Director in a St. Ignace Lumber firm. By the way, his name wasn't really Michelson, it was instead, Mickelson with a K instead of the H. The Michelson family name change occurred when a clerk for his lumber mill ordered business stationary with the name Mickelson misspelled. The young company needed the stationary and it seemed easier to Nels to use the paper instead of wasting it. His name has been spelled Michelson ever since.

Margarethe died in 1893 at age 40. In her memory, Nels contributed money for the building of a church that became the Michelson Memorial Methodist Episcopal Church of Grayling.

Nels Mickelson   Margrethe Mickelson

By the mid 1890's the largest part of the lumber boom in both Roscommon and Crawford Counties was past and the large lumbering firms had moved on to other areas. The Salling-Hansen Company participated in the move; the firm opened a lumber operation in Monroe, Louisiana in 1906.

Nels had always been interested in farming and he decided to buy a farm in Roscommon County, the former Hall farm along the western shore of Houghton Lake. He bought the farm and immediately began expanding the operation to create a sizeable stock farm with 600 cattle and 200 sheep. As he surveyed the land around his farm, Michelson decided there was still money to be earned in Roscommon logging and by using a variety of timber rather than only cutting white pine. Consequently, his 1895 purchase of seven thousand acres of land in Roscommon became only the beginning; he added to this acreage until he had about fifty thousand acres in Roscommon and Missaukee counties. In 1908 he organized the N. Michelson Lumber Company and built two large mills, a saw mill and shingle mill. His son, Axel Michelson became the General Manager of the operation at a settlement that soon earned the name of Michelson, Michigan. The little town and the logging operations were supported by a railroad, The Grand Rapids & Indiana Railroad Co. that established a branch line to Michelson.

The village of Michelson was built just after the mills were finished and was located due west of Houghton Lake at the current site of the Reedsburg Dam Flooding area. Only then, there was no flooding, the Muskegon River was a wide, clear stream of fast running water with its beginning less than a mile away at Houghton Lake. The Michelson mills were steam operated with high stacks towering above the nearest trees. Nearby were the houses, all painted white along a dusty street called Main Street. The town had a general store, a school, boarding house, and dance hall. At its heyday, 500 people called Michelson, Michigan their home town.

In 1912 Nels Michelson decided there were opportunities in real estate in Detroit. He organized the Michelson Land & Home Company, which purchased over one thousand acres of land joining the city limits on Woodward Avenue. His purchase was just in time: the city grew from some four hundred thousand people to over a million in the course of a few years. The consequence of his real estate investments in Detroit added immeasurably to his wealth.

Michelson retired to Detroit and built a beautiful large home in the tony section of the city, on Boston Ave. The home featured large, ornate rooms with hand carved artifacts made from exotic woods. The home became a part of the Detroit music scene when Berry Gordy of Motown Records purchased it.

The Boston – Edison Neighborhood Home of Nels Michelson

Another legacy of Michelson came from his oldest daughter Karen. While the young lady lived with her parents in Grayling, Michigan, she met and married into the family of one of the area's first settlers, the Hartwick family. Her young husband, Edward E. Hartwick enlisted in the army before the outbreak of World War I and quickly became an officer, attaining the rank of Major. During the war, the young man became a casualty of the American effort in France, never returning home.

Karen used some of her assets to purchase 8,000 acres of land from The Salling-Hanson Company that she then donated to the State as a memorial park to be named for her husband. The acreage included 85 acres of old growth white pine. Also wishing to commemorate the logging history of the region and of her family, Karen Hartwick requested that the Hartwick Pines Logging Museum be built in the park.

She was also involved in the naming of two of the park's lakes. Her father had a team of oxen which he used for skidding logs out of the forest during his early years. The animals were named Bright and Star and Karen suggested that the former Alexander Lakes be renamed in their honor. The state board of geographic names felt that there were already too many Star Lakes in Michigan, but they settled on Glory instead, thus Hartwick Pines' Bright Lake and Glory Lake have forever immortalized two oxen used in the early logging days.

Lumbermen had arrived in Roscommon from a variety of places beginning in the early 1870's. As the decade wore on the lumbering operations became more sophisticated and commanded more support from railroads. One of the developments that promoted logging was the introduction of railroad spurs (shorter tracks from a mainline) from railroads other than the Michigan Central. One important spur came from Meredith along the present route of M-18 to Houghton Lake. At a point six miles south of Houghton Lake the track split: one spur went west to Boyce Lake, another east to Headquarters Lake, and a third north to Houghton Lake. This point was known as the "Y".

Each of the spurs headed toward a lumber camp. The section of track that came to Houghton Lake went directly onto the lake via a 2,000 foot trestle where logs were dumped into the lake for their long trip to Muskegon via the Muskegon River.

The arrival of the railroad to the forested areas brought many changes in lumbering methods. Prime tracts of remote timber became accessible when private companies built railroads to the timber. Logs were loaded on flat cars and small locomotives pulled the flat cars to the nearest rollaway where the logs were dumped into rivers and lakes. The Muskegon Booming Company, developed to drive the logs downriver, made the river drive downstream to the owner's mills in Muskegon much more efficient. These drives down the Muskegon were a vital part of Roscommon logging on the west side of the county.

The most important lumberman who came to work the forests on the west side to the county was also the wealthiest, Ammi Willard Wright. Wright (1822 to 1912) earned his fortune early in the lumber business and then expanded it further by investments in other businesses and financial institutions. During the days when wages were $1 per day for the shanty boys, Wright became first a millionaire and then later was said to be worth more than $100 million, a phenomenal sum in those days.

AMMI WILLARD WRIGHT

Wright was born in Vermont in 1822 and learned the value of hard work as a young man when he spent 3 years farming followed by two years of work running a hotel. Like many other Americans he decided to seek his fortune in the west and so he came to Detroit in 1850 and then moved to the small town of Saginaw where he became a land-looker and selected pine lands for himself along the Cass River. He then joined forces with two other men and began lumbering operations, purchasing their own saw mill.

The venture was very successful and allowed Wright to expand his reach in the lumber business by purchasing land in Otsego County along a lake which soon bore his name. In partnership with two other men, Wright purchased land in Minnesota totaling some 70,000 acres which he sold in 1892 to Frederick Weyerhauser. However, he retained mineral rights for 20,000 acres which was subsequently found to contain iron – the land was a part of the fabled Mesaba Iron Range. Wright also found time to purchase land in Roscommon, Gladwin and Clare Counties and established an extensive lumbering operation including a railroad line to carry logs. He was one of the organizers of the Tittabawassee Boom Company where he became one of the Directors of the firm and then its President.

Wright's obvious success and wealth from the lumbering business prompted other businessmen to seek his counsel and help. The result was that Wright was asked to manage The First National Bank of Saginaw and he became its President. In time, he also took on the Presidency of several other banks: the Merchants National Bank of Duluth, the Commercial Bank of Mt. Pleasant, and the Merchants Bank of Battle Creek. Probably as a result of his banking business, Wright became a successful investor and he took positions in many companies including Michigan Sugar, Alma Manufacturing, and Portland Cement of Union City.

Ammi had a lifelong interest in farming so he purchased a large farm in Gratiot County near Alma, Michigan where he actively engaged in farming. His boundless energy soon became evident in Alma when he decided to improve things by building a 'model city.' The result was that he built Opera House Block, an assemblage of stores, a three-story hotel, the Alma Flouring mill and the Alma Creamery. He also began Alma College and the Alma Sanitarium and he constructed a beautiful home in Alma as well. He died at this home in 1892 at the age of 89 leaving his 2nd wife and his only daughter.

The Wright Hotel in Alma, Built by Ammi Wright

By the late 1870's, Roscommon County seemed like a flame attracting moths on a summer night as lumbermen flocked to the area for the virgin pine. In a few short years after the railroad arrived, the quiet forests resounded with the sounds of axes, saws and men working. Lumbermen and lumber camps were everywhere about the county: around the lakes, at each river, and at each of the smallest streams that led to a lake or river. In addition to the names of Stephens, Michelson and Wright, Roscommon County residents soon began hearing the names of other lumbermen who were operating camps. The larger ones that commanded the most attention were the brothers A.H. Gerrish and W. S. Gerrish, the large firm of Blodgett & Byrne, the individual operators Thomas Nester, B. Geel, John Murray, H. Moore, Wm. Terney and a company that became a large operation mostly on the west side of the county, The Roscommon Lumber Co.

A Pinery in the North Woods Before the Lumbermen Came

The most sought-after logs that lumbermen were seeking were large white and red pines that grew in stands the lumbermen called pineries. The stands varied in size but all were valuable as each contained large virgin trees that contained the most board feet and commanded the highest prices.

By 1880, Roscommon lumbering operations were in full flower and the men in control were growing wealthy or wealthier. The county prospered as well as jobs were plentiful and businesses were straining to satisfy demands for just about everything that men and women and children needed to lead productive lives. A regular boom was on.

Chapter 8

First Settlers and Villages

The first settlement in Roscommon County occurred in 1871 when a few farm families converged on a spot along the south shore of the biggest lake in the county. The settlement was called Edna and is now known as Prudenville. Shortly after, Roscommon Station and St. Helens were settled as result of the railroad. The settlement at Houghton Lake also sprouted in 1872 without benefit of a railroad nearby.

The railroad needed stations at close distances in order for the hungry steam engines to take on fuel (wood) and water. However, there was more to it than that: the railroad was keenly aware of the logging and lumbering business and its potential when they established their stations near waterways at a suitable distance from West Branch. The stations that were built at each site had a depot and station master who could arrange for shipments of goods and lumber, although in the very beginning there was little need at either station as commerce in the area was virtually non-existent.

The St. Helens station was named after the adjacent lake of St. Helens. Some say that the name came from a Frenchman that the railroad and The Henry Stephens Lumber Co. folks found living near the lake. Apparently, they understood his name was St. Helen and they referred to the big lake as if it were his – St. Helen's. They promised to name the lake after him providing that he would move to make room for their operations. According to other folks, the lake was named after Baron St. Helens, an Irish nobleman known to the Irish surveyor of the district, John Brink.

[Author's note - Brink's survey map in 1841 and Burt's map in 1852 left the lake unnamed. Furthermore, inspection of the Surveyor's Field Notes makes no mention

of the name of the lake. An account of a camping trip to the lake in 1871 indicates that the lake was unnamed then. Accordingly, I favor the opinion that the railroad used the name because of a Frenchmen they found trapping near the lake].

Roscommon Station was named after the County that was officially named Roscommon by legislator Charley O'Malley who convinced the state legislature to adopt that name in 1843.

In consequence of the forests and the Stephens Company lumbering all around the new station of St. Helens, a tiny village grew to supply the railroad, its passengers and the nearby lumber camps. The post office at St. Helens was established in 1874 with Mrs. Louise Tebo as the first postmaster. Louise promptly changed the name of the post office from St. Helens to St. Helen, dropping the last S. The new name stuck and the village came to be known by the name of the post office, no matter what the state thought or the maps showed.

Only a few widely scattered farms existed over the County when Louise changed the name of the Post Office. One of the earliest farm families who lived north of St. Helen (but which was then included in Richfield Township) were the Richardson's, who arrived in 1875 and homesteaded on land in the northeast part of the county (now Au Sable Township). The Richardson family donated land for a school and the school building was moved nearly 100 years later and is now displayed by the Roscommon Historical Society in the village of Roscommon.

The first known settler to the area near Lake St. Helen was a man named Jake Throop. *The Roscommon News* said that Throop settled in the area in 1869 when it was an unbroken wilderness. Throop evidently spent his time as a trapper and hunter prompting the *News* to comment on his prowess at those endeavors. Notwithstanding the *News* report, four young men spent the winter of 1871 (*A Winter in the Pine Woods*, C. A. Wean) around the lake hunting for animals for their pelts and they failed to come across Throop. The young men also commented that the lake was unnamed and so they used their own name, Bear Lake, for the bear they encountered while crossing it in an Indian dugout they had found on the shore.

The village of St. Helen owed its existence to The Henry Stephens Lumber Co. and the railroad. Even during its heyday, the village businesses were few and the population small: The Michigan State Gazatteer listed a population of 200 people during the height of the lumber boom. When the Stephens Company closed their operations in the County, the village nearly disappeared.

Michigan Central Railroad Station at Roscommon

Roscommon Station came into being soon after St. Helen when the railroad built that station along the banks of the South Branch of the Au Sable. Like St. Helen, the area was surrounded by forests and the potential for the lumbering and logging business was well known to the railroad line. The railroad built a small station, hired an agent and began advertising for travelers and freight to the remote area. The travelers, of course, needed a place to stay and so two hotels promptly sprouted, The Pioneer House (still remaining and known as the Spruce Motor Lodge) and The Dougherty

Hotel. The Pioneer House was built in late 1872 and operated by a woman, Ms. Ursule Mercier, who had the distinction of being one of Roscommon Station's earliest residents.

Believed to be the First Roscommon Hotel in 1873
(Photo from Roscommon Centennial Publication. This must have been Ursule Mericer's hotel that was described as a 1 and ½ story hotel)

One of the early arrivals to Roscommon Station was a young lawyer by the name of George O. Robinson. Robinson owned a law firm in Detroit in partnership with another attorney, David Brooks. Robinson was a respected attorney and a patriot, a member of Sons of the Revolution by virtue of his grandfather's service in the Revolutionary War. He was also an ambitious man with an eye for new business adventures. Somehow, he and Brooks had learned about real estate opportunities in Roscommon and so he decided to visit the territory and see for himself. He arrived at the new station and was delighted to learn there was still land for sale – not just any land, but land all around the area where the new railroad station had been built. Robinson consulted with Brooks and the two agreed that Roscommon Station provided a wonderful opportunity for a new real estate business.

In the warm summer of 1872, Robinson began buying land, much of it still for sale from the U. S. government since no one had yet purchased it. In

July, August and Sept. he negotiated the purchase of several tracts of land, 1043 acres in total, at rock bottom prices in various sections of the county. He made the first purchases in partnership with Brooks, but later he purchased land in his name only.

Robinson and Brooks conferred about the new opportunity and decided that Robinson would pursue this opportunity while Brooks returned to Detroit to manage their law firm. Accordingly, Robinson and his wife Helen built a home in the frontier area which served as a real estate office. He then began the task of convincing new arrivals from the railroad that there were opportunities in Roscommon and a good place to start was the purchase of land from Robinson and Brooks, Realtors. Business must have been slow at first, but growth was on the way. The respected Michigan State Gazetteer & Business Directory had their first listing for Roscommon Station in 1875.

MICHIGAN

STATE GAZETTEER

AND

BUSINESS DIRECTORY

FOR 1875.

R. L. POLK & CO., Compilers.

PRICE FIVE DOLLARS

DETROIT.
THE TRIBUNE PRINTING COMPANY

The Gazetteer listed the following Roscommon businesses in 1875:

Business Directory
Station Agent ....S. Bennett
General Store..............Bennett Bros.
Physician & Hotel ....S. Derby
Hotel......................J. J. Pierson
Hotel......................J. Raizon
General Store..............John Trask

The south end of the county soon hosted its own villages of Houghton Lake and Edna. These came shortly before and after Roscommon Station and St. Helen and were fueled by the arrival of settlers intent on making a new life in the wilderness area. Edna (now Prudenville) was the county's first village beginning in 1871 and it grew at the place where Denton Creek emptied into Houghton Lake. It took the name of Edna for Edna Denton who became the first postmistress. Houghton Lake was settled in 1873 shortly after Roscommon Station was built.

One of the first farmers to the south part of Roscommon County who became a permanent resident was Augustus Emory and his family. Augustus, his wife and seven children left Chesaning, Mi. in the spring of 1873 and headed north on the Saginaw Trail. They stopped at Edenville along the Tittabawassee River and then followed the northwest fork of the trail toward Houghton Lake. The boys of the family walked, driving their cattle, while Augustus drove the wagon that carried his wife and daughters and their tools and meager household goods. At a point three miles south of the lake and near the present M18 highway, the family found a spot on a ridge above a stream to build a house and barn. Augustus and his three grown sons, Augustus Jr., 21, William, 19, and Harvey, 17, began the difficult job of cutting some of the giant white pines for lumber for the house and barn on the 160 acre property.

They built a log house and made a roof from hand-split cedar shingles. They left openings for windows and covered the square opening with skins that were scraped clean of fur and oiled to let light in. The open fireplace served for heating and cooking and the rough sawn planks made the floor. A granddaughter remembers visiting her grandma and noticing that she never needed a dustpan when she swept the floor since the planks had enough spaces between them to capture all the dust.

Shortly after the Emory's arrived, two other families followed: Albert Wickham and his family and Sam Stickney and his family. Wickham said that Augustus had beaten him to Roscommon by 30 days; otherwise he would have been first. The Emory's, Wickham's and Stickney's all homesteaded due south of Prudenville, intent on making a living by farming after first clearing the land and using or selling the timber. Many of the Roscommon pioneers were related or acquainted when they came to Roscommon to begin a new life. Here is an abridged version of the story published in the Houghton Lake News in the 1960's concerning several early Roscommon pioneers. The account was written by John Charles Wickham, grandson of Albert Wickham.

"My granddad, Albert R. Wickham, first came to Houghton Lake in the year 1868. He was land-looking for a quarter section of land with the valuable Cork Pine, as he called it. The Norway or Red Pine was also in demand as masts for sailing ships. Born on an island in the Maumee River, south of Toledo, Ohio, Albert R. Wickham and his brother John C. Wickham, who was two years older (born 1842 and 1844, respectively) were the sons of George Wickham and wife, Lydia Cox. Albert and John answered President Lincoln's call for volunteers in 1861, along with two cousins, William Hale (later to be Roscommon County's first Judge of Probate) and Layfayette Hale. The volunteers also included a neighbor boy, Alfred Wilson, who later married a Wickham girl. He was the fireman in the great train robbery, a suicidal attempt to end the Civil War, when a spy and Union soldier started a locomotive and raced into the South tearing rails and burning bridges.

123

Along with another cousin, Noah Cox, all enlisted in the 21st Ohio Volunteers. Noah lost his sight at Missionary Ridge, but lived to be a father of eleven children. There was also a small middle-aged gunsmith in the army from Wood County, Ohio, William Stocking and his wife Mary Lamb Stocking. All these people followed my granddad to Roscommon County to take advantage of a quarter section of free land (160 acres) for veterans, under the Homestead Act as did the fathers of the Owen and Knapp families.

John and Albert and the entire command of the 21st Ohio were captured at the battle of Chickamauga Creek. They spent two years and ten months in seven southern prisons including Libby, Andersonville, Richmond and Danville. John and twenty-three others tunneled out of the Danville, Virginia prison. Albert, too weak to walk, lay on rotten blankets covering the hole. All were recaptured, except John and two others. John and his two companions hid out from the Confederates in the woods, making their way north by night. They spent twenty-one day in the wilds of West Virginia, approaching slave quarters for food that was readily given. After a harrowing and exhausting trip he made it to the Union lines. A month later, Albert was released on a prisoner exchange and sent home. He was in delicate health for some years thereafter.

During the war, John and Albert were privates and detailed to help the gunsmith Stocking. He took a liking to the boys and told them, "I've got two pretty daughters at home, single, and both have something wrong with them. Come see us when this war is over." Well, John and Albert did just that. The boys looked their brides over for many moons before they discovered the defects in the young ladies and both decided the problems weren't worth worrying about. John married Sadie and Albert married Mary.

The defects? Sadie had been born deaf in one ear. She had a happy life for many years in Roscommon before she died at Summit Heights, Houghton Lake about 1940. Albert, my granddad, married Mary, blind in one eye. She had stood on a block of wood in school sharpening a pencil with a pen knife, when the block rolled and she put her eye out. She had been fitted with a glass eye, and as a joke on the boys, the girl's secrets were kept by all.

After the boys were married, they settled down to a life near Toledo. Albert soon fathered two daughters, Mae and Sadie. Albert's wife Mary fell ill of consumption. Albert took Mary to his Army Colonel, a famous doctor in Cincinnati. After a complete examination, he told Albert he was going to lose Mary soon if he didn't move from Toledo to a dryer place. Before they left Cincinnati for home, a council of war was held at the home of Colonel Kapplan. The Colonel said, "Boy's, I was on a hunting trip with a college friend by the name of Houghton, two years ago. The State of Michigan has built a road from Saginaw Bay, northwest to Traverse Bay. My friend helped on the survey and they named a big lake after him, it's about 100 miles north of Saginaw. The hunting and fishing is the best I ever saw and Virgin Pine line the south shore. The big lake is a paradise. Now, Albert, here is my advice, sell your meat business in Toledo, homestead a quarter section of Pine, get as close to the lake as possible. As it's the headwaters of the Muskegon River, logs can be driven downriver. Some company will come there and start a big operation, have your logs banked on the shore and they will buy them. Go find the piece you want, build a camp on it. As for Mary she must have complete rest, your girls are big enough to help some. Make her a pillow of Pine needles, also a mattress. Complete rest and my medicine are her only hope. Boy's, I'll help with money and medicine, and come to see her as often as I can. (An excuse to go fishing.)

So granddad sold his meat business to his brother John, and went to work for Captain Canfield, buying and delivering big draft horses to camps near Lansing and Midland. He managed three or four teams at a time, riding one and leading the others. After several years of this, he was able to come to the lake with a borrowed team. He fixed his camp at what is known as Five Points, Denton Township, north of the Baptist Church at Owens Lake. Granddad was ready to move in 1869, but Mary was very weak, and to complicate things, pregnant. Well, they started anyway, travelling slowly. At Diamondale, Michigan she could go no farther. So at a big lumber camp on Snow Lake he went to work as a cook. The boss was a veteran of

Missionary Ridge, and he fixed a nice shanty for Mary and her daughters. There in the shanty on Snow Lake on September 25, 1870, my dad, a little red-headed boy was born to Mary and Albert. They named him William Case Wickham. The men in camp were all happy for Mary and her son, and when the Diamondale doctor gave the "all's well", they went on a toot that landed a good number of them in jail in Eaton Rapids.

Mary was too weak to leave for Houghton Lake for 18 months. During that time granddad made trips to their homestead and built a barn for oxen. Finally, in the spring of 1872 Mary and children were ready to travel and the family was able to settle on their homestead near Nester Hills (now Mid-Forest Lodge). In the spring of 1872, granddad got in a huge garden and a field of corn and taters. By the spring of '73 Mary's lungs had improved and they had a visit from the Colonel doctor. He knew by Mary's letter that her eye was failing, so he brought a kit and fitted her to glasses. Then he gave Mary a lecture. He said, "Mary, your folks gave you a mighty fine education, even public speaking on account of your eye accident. Now, you are the best read woman in the north, you must teach Albert to read and write. He had to make an X when he enlisted. You must start a school and a Sunday school. This settlement will grow so you will have to keep timber records for yourself and the neighbors or they will be cheated. These things you can and must do. Hell, Mary, you are no dead weight -- you have to be boss of this outfit." And she was, till her dying day.

Granddad took to figures later in life, bought and shipped sheep, cattle and hogs to Detroit and Buffalo. He also studied public speaking and law. He was Under-sheriff a lot and had a shingle out in the yard. I remember[it]; A.R. Wickham, Auctioneer, and how he loved to cry and sell. In the spring of '75, an old army buddy and his relation moved to Houghton Lake and settled on homesteads; The Hale's and Blind Noah Cox, with a big brood of children. Each following spring brought more settlers.

Mary's lungs were still healing but she was still boss and everyone helped each other. She wrote letters and did figures for backwoods boys and girls. Lumberjacks hoed her sweet corn, and in return she would write to their folks. There was always company at their modest house and Mary couldn't get travelling Indians to help her even though they were always begging meat and potatoes. Young Bill Emory grew like a weed, and he brought Mary many deer. When the Prudden's came to East Bay, Prudden hired granddad to cut and skid logs. Bill Emory went along to drive the oxen and hook chains. He was very young, but tall and strong and he became an expert hunter and trapper.

Granddad took a job cutting meat in Roscommon during the winter months so the girls could get some schooling. In the spring, Dad said he and another kid caught Grayling White Trout in the creek by William's Gas Station, which is now Roscommon Village. They took the fish to a hotel outside of town, and some fancy ladies bought them. They gave the boys candy, soft drinks, and a big price, which was more than they got at the meat market. But they got caught! Mary found out and gave her red-headed son Willie, a whippin' and made him promise he would never go near a place like that again. Granddad said, "don't make my boy swear to a lie."

Somehow granddad got a skid-road built to lake shore. It was the first road to Houghton Lake. I asked granddad how he got so much done with no money to hire help. He said, "It seemed like folks always owed us something". Mary did a lot of nursing; the Colonel gave her some needles, medicine, and medical books so Mary set broken arms or legs no matter how much people yelled because of the pain. Nobody had any money, but she had a way of making folks work and pay us back." When Ole Pluckett got his shoulder chewed by a bear, Mary kept him for weeks, but he was too old to work. She wouldn't dream of letting him pay her. Each year granddad's clearing grew. Things were looking up as Mary was on the mend, besides her father and mother left Toledo, Ohio for Houghton Lake Village. Grandfather Stocking would open a gun shop and wagon works there. Then disaster struck again in Camp 16, which is now Edenville, Michigan. Some half-breed French and Indians stole Granddad Stocking's boat, and his beloved tools for rifling, etc. Someone told him in time and he borrowed a rifle and shot the fellow poling the boat in the thigh. He recovered his property but the culprit died some weeks later going down *river on a raft. A US Marshall arrested granddad for murder in the 1st degree with no bail and returned him to the Edenville jail, which was Camp 16 then. So to get his father-in-law (William C. Stocking) freed, Albert Rosewell Wickham sold his team of oxen yoke and chains to Ole Prudden, his employer at that time. He walked to Saginaw and hired a young red-haired lawyer just out of law school. After hearing Albert's story, the lawyer said, "I'll free him for $100. I'll prove he died of neglect and that those mustard plasters caused the gangarene." He won and Albert had his hot-headed father-in-law back, but no oxen.*

All judicial matters at that time were handled at the Midland County Court House some 65 miles distant. It was said that the walk to Midland from Roscommon took two and one half days. The judge who heard the case was accustomed to the rambunctious behavior of lumberjacks. He decided that Stocking was not guilty since he was only defending his property. The logging men who had come to watch the trial for entertainment evidently agreed with the judge because they broke into cheers when the judge rendered his verdict and hoisted Stocking on their shoulder for a trip to the nearest saloon. Stocking celebrated his victory by sitting on the saloon bar and playing a fiddle for the rest of the night while the crowd of men danced and drank. The next morning the tired Stocking began his 65 mile walk home.

The big break came the following spring. Stephen S. Hall came to the head of the lake with a camp of sixty-five men and settled on the bluff which is Houghton Heights now. At that time, there were some big dugout canoes on the lake, left by Indians. The settlers polled the canoes over to the Muskeogon River and down river to a marsh hay. After waiting for a good Northwester to blow, they would push out from shore for a wild ride to Denton Pt. and Johnson's Indian Village to stack their hay for the winter.

Granddad heard of the big camp at Muddy River, he said, "Boy's, we'll give 'em a mess of fish." So they gathered on the Norway Pine Patch and put wagon boxes across canoes with a large iron basket in front. One dark, quiet spring night they set forth with two men poling and two spearing. At dawn they were pulled up in front of Stephen Hall's camp with a load of fresh fish. Hall was delighted and said, Boy's, I'll give you barreled salt pork, pound for pound." Granddad often said of all my dealing, that was the best deal I ever made; because when the girls boiled potatoes, they put enough salt pork in to do the job and had salt left in the barrel for the stock. No more ox cart trips to Midland. Shortly after, Mr. Hall called granddad and said, "Folks, I didn't know a settlement was so near. I'll buy every tater, onion, carrot, turnip and cabbage you can raise; and pay you with cash or goods. I'll hire your teams in the winter, too. Wickham, I want your logs at once." He even gave granddad cash in advance. Granddad went south and bought two big teams of horses this time with sleighs and wagons. One wagon was a sprinkler, a gift from his old boss at Snow Lake. Granddad's logging business went ahead but his bladder troubles got worse. An old Indian medicine man had the squaws gather roots and bark, Juniper and Balsam. It was bitter to take, but it cured him. Mary sent the good old Colonel Doctor some, for he had been a prisoner, too.

In the year 1877, there was a school house at Five Points. The first pupils were Fred Hale, Etta Hale, Mae Wickham, Sadie Wickham, William Wickham, Sophia Cox, and Tom Cox. About this time, the Colonel applied for John and Albert Wickham and got them $8.00 a month pensions. Other settlers came fast now. Grandmother's lungs were healed and she wanted to go back to Ohio where her pretty daughters wouldn't have to marry illiterate lumberjacks. Granddad and Grandma finally sold out and moved to Toledo. In 1909, my grandparents returned to Houghton Lake and bought twelve acres across from the Pines Theater. They lived the rest of their lives in Northern Michigan.

Activity began on the western end of the lake when a few families arrived shortly after the Wickham's and Stickney's. These pioneers, the Lawton Knapp's, Eugene Kemp's, and Edward Nelson's, all travelled north on the Harrison Trail and stopped to homestead within sight of the lake.

Like other of the early farmers and settlers in the north woods, the Emory's and other early settlers spent much of the summer in the outdoors since most of their work involved outdoor activities. The outdoor work included household tasks such as washing the clothes. Here are the instructions for washing clothes that was carefully written for the benefit of a new bride:

1. *Bild a fire in the back yard to heet a kettle of rain water.*
2. *Set tubs so wind won't blow in eyes if the wind is pert.*
3. *Shave on hole cake of soap in bilin water*
4. *Sort things, make three piles, 1 pile white, 1 pile cullored, 1 pile work britches and rags.*
5. *Stur starch in cold water to smooth, then thin down with bilin water.*
6. *Rub dirty spots on board, scrub hard, then bile, rub cullored but don't bile.*
7. *Take white things out of kettle with broom handle, then rench, blew and starch.*
8. *Spred tee towels on grass.*
9. *Hang old rags on fence.*
10. *Pore rench water on flower beds.*
11. *Scrub porch with soapy water.*
12. *Turn tubs upside down.*
13. *Go put on cleen dress, smooth hair with combs, brew a cup of tea, sit and rest and rock for a spell and count blessins.*

Many of the farmers that came to Roscommon County and most of the shanty boys arrived from the south. The nearest large lumber operations to the south were at Edenville and Red Keg, both camps along the Tittabawassee in Midland County. Red Keg was particularly noteworthy as the camp and then the village took its name from the most important saloon in the area, The Red Keg. (The village is now known as Averill.) As the remote areas became settled, civilization took an occasional odd turn as justice was meted out in the fastest, most efficient way possible. Here is one of many stories about justice in Red Keg.

"A case of lumberjack justice was told concerning Billy McCrary who ran the famous Red Keg saloon in the 1870's. McCrary became vexed at the actions of one of his customers and beat up on the man with no apparent justification. The village constable observed the assault and declared Mc

Crary under arrest. When he started to escort him to the nearest justice, 'Swearin' Charlie Axford, owner of a hotel and saloon at camp 16 often called the 'Mayor of Edenville' stepped forward. " 'What are you taking him to the Justice of the Peace for? Try him before me. I am in business and can hold court as well as anybody.' "

Both parties agreed and adjourned to a nearby hotel. 'Stand up, Bill,' Axford said. 'Are you guilty or not guilty?'

'Guilty, your honor,' McCrary said smiling.

'I hereby fine you $3 cash and whiskey for the crowd!' Axford decreed. 'We will now adjourn to the Red Keg and collect the fine and costs.' "

And so was justice meted out in the north woods in its earliest days. Saloons often served as the center of activity in the outpost areas where neighbors were few and far between and a saloon was the nearest thing to civilization. Beer and whiskey were the drinks of choice for most of the saloon crowd and for a time, Detroit with its German immigrants bragged of its unequalled brewing capacity.

After the Emory's arrived in Roscommon in 1873, a few more farmers settled in the south end of the county in 1874 and 1875. By then there were enough families scattered around the southern part of the county and at Houghton Lake to support small settlements. The Michigan State Gazatteer reported that Edna (now known as Prudenville) was settled first with a few farmers gathering to make an established settlement in 1871. It grew slowly; by 1877, the settlement could count only 50 people and there were but 20 people reported at Houghton Lake at the same date. The Gazatteer said the village of Houghton Lake was settled in 1873 on the shores of *Roscommon Lake.* Lumbering was said to be the sole industry in Houghton Lake whereas Edna shipped fur and fish to market in 1877. Mrs.

Denton was post mistress in Edna and the attorney H. H. Woodruff served the same function in Houghton Lake.

Even though the villages were small and the outlying areas were sparsely settled, residents began talking about the need for home rule. Some liked to argue that having their own county offices would eliminate the need for travel to Midland and make things a lot simpler (Midland County handled all administrative matters for Roscommon County until 1875). Accordingly, a few men made inquiries with the state about how they could manage to have their own independent county offices and officials. Their inquiries led to a chain of events that ultimately resulted in the development of new county offices for Roscommon (see chapter 9).

The railroad opened the north woods to the world. Suddenly the county's unknown, remote areas with its beautiful lakes and streams became known and admired to people from distant places. By riding the train, It became possible to reach the county from places like Detroit, hundreds of miles to the south. And the Michigan Central made sure that travelers knew about the popular places where the train stopped. The Au Sable River in particular, gained the attention of fishermen and hunters as parties of sportsmen paddled up and down the stream in search of game. Stories in 1878 and 1879 in The Detroit Free Press and in Scribner's Monthly (1878) about deer hunting and fishing on the Au Sable and those Grayling Trout added immeasurably to the cachet of the area.

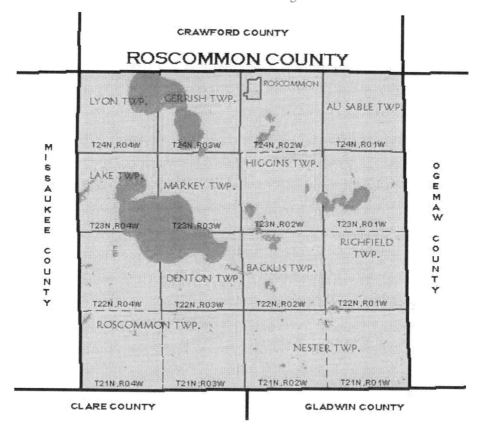

Roscommon County Map (http//Michigan.gov/cgi) **Township and Ranges**

The first legislative townships were Roscommon, Denton and Higgins. As the county grew, additional townships were set off from the original three ultimately leading to the current 11 townships shown on the map.

In the late 1870's it took about as long to reach Roscommon from Edna or Houghton Lake as it did to reach Roscommon from Detroit. The Michigan Central ran either one or two trains to Roscommon each day in addition to

133

special excursions to Bay City or other locations. It was common for Roscommon residents to take a relaxing train ride for a one day or overnight excursion. But if you lived in Edna and needed to go to Roscommon for a day's business, you were in for a long, tiring day. You might take a horse and wagon or, if you were in a hurry, you would walk as the road from Edna to Roscommon was exceedingly bad. Depending upon the recent weather, the road might be impassable for a horse and buggy since a good part of the way was through a wetlands area where the road often became a muck filled bog. Most times the road was bad and those with buggies had to make long detours to avoid getting stuck.

"Harvey Emory was known as a great walker and one day he was walking to Roscommon when he came upon a neighbor, Tom Knight, also on his way to Roscommon with a team and wagon. Tom said, 'Hop on and ride, Harvey.' Harvey replied, ' Can't do it, I'm in a hurry.'

Harvey went on his way, did his business in Roscommon, ate lunch and was returning home when he met Tom with his wagon still on his way to Roscommon."

The road between Houghton Lake and Roscommon remained an unimproved dirt, sand and muck trail for several years until lumber companies improved the road by creating a corduroy road through the wet areas. These 'logways' were created by laying down six inch diameter logs, side by side, then covering them with brush and smaller poles before coating the entire assemblage with a layer of dirt. The 'logways' made a passable road when it was new but it soon became a bumpy, washboard surface when the dirt washed away in the spring rains and left the logs exposed. It wasn't until the road surface was built up with thick layers of gravel that the road became a smooth, comfortable passageway.

Edna, Houghton Lake, St. Helen and the former Roscommon Station which became Roscommon, were the primary villages of the county in the 1870's.

The men and women who laid claim to Roscommon land totaled only several hundred people, mostly farmers, with the notable exception of lumbermen who purchased large chunks of Roscommon County land for logging. The real estate business became profitable and busy as lumber barons bargained for the best available lands of pine. The spin-off from them created demand for smaller parcels of land for those who worked in the lumber business. The result was an active real estate business.

One of those who dealt in real estate around Prudenville was John E. Harcourt, a wheeler –dealer and prolific parent of six sons. Harcourt built a hotel in almost the center of Edna to handle the influx of new residents who were interested in the lumber business that was rapidly becoming all pervasive in the county. Even farmers in the area became involved in the lumber business as Peter Pruden and another local man, Dresdan Bryan, opened a saw mill on the shores of Houghton Lake.

Things looked rosy for the county as business boomed and the population shot up. New people seemed to arrive daily and they began building homes of one sort or another all around the county's lumber camps that seemed as numerous as flies. What the county needed now was some effective political leaders who could keep things on an even keel what with all the changes in the wind.

Chapter 9

Politics Elections & Growth

The State of Michigan and Roscommon County grew out of The Northwest Ordinance of 1787. This remarkable law passed by the new United States Congress, authored in part by Thomas Jefferson, provided for a survey system that envisioned local government based on counties and townships in those counties. The townships were six miles square, each containing 36 sections of land, with 16 townships per county.

Legislative townships as defined by the law were different from the survey townships: legislative townships were political subdivisions of the county for the purpose of creating local government units. If the townships defined by the survey system had a large enough population, then they could serve as the legislative township as well. If the population in the townships was not large, then legislative townships could be defined that were different than the six mile square townships defined by survey. When Roscommon County was created be the State in 1875, it was recognized that the population was too small to have 16 units of government, thus new legislative townships were defined by combining several survey townships.

In the beginning it was agreed that three townships would be sufficient to serve the small, but growing population. The three legislative townships were given the same name as the two largest lakes, Roscommon and Higgins, and the third township was named after a family who were instrumental in organizing the township and county, the Denton's.

Albert and Elizabeth Denton and their three children had come to Roscommon early along with several others of the Denton family. The 26 year old Denton described himself as a lumberman and he came to take advantage of the big trees that were right where he settled. Neighbors living near the Denton's were Peter Pruden and his wife Catherine, Dresdan and Mary Byran and others who were all to figure in the development of the County.

The Denton's lived along a small creek (now known as Denton Creek) that flowed into Houghton Lake at the former site of the Indian village along the lake. Albert immediately recognized that if he were able to dam the creek, he could create enough water flow to carry his logs to the lake for sawing or for further transport to the Muskegon River. Before long, the Denton's had developed a system of seven dams along the small creek to carry logs from a number of points upstream.

By 1875 enough settlers had moved to the County so that the State was willing to recognize a local unit of government for Roscommon County instead of requiring all legal matters be handled at Midland. The citizens were advised to meet and organize before holding elections for township officials. Thus, several of the leading citizens arranged a meeting of all eligible voters in the county. The meeting was held at the largest home in the area, the Hall farm near Houghton Lake Village on April 5, 1875. The meeting was convened with 152 men from the area (females were not yet allowed to vote) who decided to seek legal status from the state based on three townships to be known as Roscommon, Denton and Higgins. Representatives for each township were nominated and asked to arrange township elections for both township and county officials.

Albert Denton was one of the instigators for home rule and so he volunteered to hold the Denton Township organizational meeting in his home on June 5, 1875. The men attending the meeting made a count of Denton Township residents and found there were 150 total residents living in the township, probably the most populous at the time. An election was held to name township officers and the following were elected;

Supervisor – F. Bradley Denton   Clerk - John Denton

Treasurer – Augustus Emory   Constable – Chas Denton

Highway Commisioner Chas Denton   Justice of the Peace –P. Pruden

Poor Master – Albert Wickham

Similar elections were held at Higgins and Roscommon Townships and their Supervisors elected. By statute, these Supervisors became the County Board of Supervisors: F. Bradley Denton from Denton Township, Daniel Burnett from Higgins, and A. P. Dickinson from Roscommon. The other officials named for the county were the following:

Sheriff   - Albert Denton   Prosecutor - Cap'n Beers

Treasurer - C. W. Stone   Clerk – Eugene Kiely

Register of Deeds – Frank Mathews   Probate Judge – Wm. Hale

The State of Michigan approved the actions of the county men and officially recognized the new county in 1875 and assigned Roscommon Station as the designated county seat. Unfortunately, Roscommon Station didn't have a single building deemed suitable for meetings of the new county officials. Consequently, it was agreed to hold official county meetings at the south end of Houghton Lake, nearer to the homes of many of the officers. The Hall farm was again suggested for use but in the end a small log schoolhouse that was on the south shore of Houghton Lake served as the meeting site. After the first meeting, The Board of Supervisors decided to make the school an all-purpose building for their meetings and for any other local government business.

The population of the new county continued to grow with farmers coming to the area and more than a few men searching for wealth in the lumber business. Most new people arriving had one thing on their minds, where can I purchase land? The land purchases meant tax revenue and that meant more business for the new local government. The Board of Supervisors decided rather quickly that a new, larger and more permanent court house was needed. The need for the new court house naturally provoked the question of where the county seat should be located.

George Robinson was aware of the political developments in the county as he platted a village around Roscommon Station in 1876 that significantly enhanced the value of his low cost lands. As soon as the plans were drawn, George shrewdly offered a free parcel of land to the Board of Supervisors for the citing of a County Courthouse. George knew that if the village became the permanent County Seat he could expect a substantial gain in his real estate business.

The Board of Supervisors wisely decided not to accept the gift until they were clear that the new village would or should become the permanent site for the Court House and thus the County Seat. Several residents felt that Roscommon Station was too far from Houghton and Edna and the roads too bad for it to become the seat of local government. Besides, both the residents of Edna and Houghton Lake wanted the court house in their village so the Board decided not to decide. The matter was brought to a head when representatives from Edna made a formal presentation to the Board on Feb 21, 1878 to have the courthouse built in their village – the largest in the county in 1878.

This bid was quickly followed by another from residents near Houghton Lake who demanded the courthouse be located on a piece of land just west of the village. The Board decided the matter was too important and too divisive for them to decide, and that it should be resolved by a vote of the electorate. Accordingly, they instructed each township to arrange an election to determine the site for the new court house.

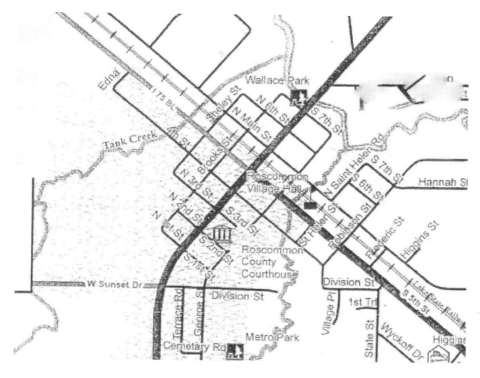

George Robinson Platted Roscommon and Chose Street Names

(George platted the village for maximum profit potential, aligning the streets to be parallel and perpendicular to the Michigan Central Railroad tracks. George didn't show much imagination in naming streets; he used his name and his partner's name for three streets (George St., Brooks St. and Robinson Street and named two others for the nearby villages of St. Helen and Edna, failing to honor the competing village of Houghton Lake with a street name. The remainder of the streets he listed as 1st through 7th. He listed his main streets as Main Street and Lake Street using the name Lake since the road led to Houghton Lake.)

Many township officials lived at or around Houghton Lake and they assumed the matter was a mere formality since the south end of the county had the most residents and Roscommon Station was still a small place some 18 miles distant. Although it was growing and it had the all-important railroad station located there, the surrounding area was not highly populated. When the vote was taken at each township and the results were tallied in April, 1878, it turned out that Roscommon Station had won the election. Houghton Lake area residents were stunned. How could it have happened? Later, it was noted that on Election Day, some 50 men arrived in Roscommon via the railroad. Did they vote for Roscommon at the bidding of the Michigan Central Railroad? At the bidding of George Robinson? Rumors swirled but no official investigation or legal action was taken because election laws at the time were lax and many voters signed their ballots with an "X" because they couldn't read or write: It would have been extremely difficult to prove anything of a fraudulent nature.

John Mahoney discussed the matter in a letter. *"They voted to move the county seat in the fall of 1878. It was moved in 1879 and Higgins Township put it over on Denton in fine shape. There was a work train with 50 men and they all voted. It was in form in them days if you gave a man a ballot and he couldn't speak his name in English, to register him as Joe Pocket. If we had too many Joe Pockets we gave them a middle name. On Election Day they all voted and Roscommon outvoted the south side of Houghton Lake."*

And so Roscommon Station (soon to be shortened to Roscommon) became the new county seat and the action was affirmed by the state in May of 1879. The County Board of Supervisors further affirmed the election results by accepting Robinson's land offer and issuing a contract for the building of a new court house. They drew up general specifications for the building to be constructed at a cost not to exceed $1,500. Local builder I. M. Silsby won the contract and began work using lumber from local sources for construction.

Roscommon County's First Court House

At their first meeting in the new building, the elected officials decided that there was a tad too much haste in the planning and construction of the new court house; there was no privy for the facility. The men quickly authorized the construction of a privy. The next order of business was almost as important as the missing privy – no one had thought to provide for the tobacco chewers. Since a majority of the adult male population used tobacco in one form or another and many used chewing tobacco, another important matter they took up was the ordering of spittoons to be strategically located about the building. After those important matters pertaining to the personal necessities of the county officers, the officials were ready to take on the county's business.

Population growth on the north and east side of the county was slower than in the south since many of the farmers came over the border from the south following the single road. Many settled near the place that the

Emory's settled – along the south side of Houghton Lake. One of the early farm families who traveled to the east side and settled north of the St. Helen Station were the Richardson's. They arrived in 1875 and homesteaded on land in the northeast part of the county (now Au Sable Township.) The Richardson family donated land for a school and the school building is now displayed by the Roscommon Historical Society.

The Michigan Central Railroad opened Michigan's north woods to the civilized world. Suddenly the county's unknown, remote areas with its beautiful lakes and streams became known and admired by people from distant places. By riding the train, It became possible to reach the county from places like Detroit or Bay City, each of which had connections to the larger world via steamboat or the Erie Canal. And the Michigan Central made sure that travelers knew about the popular places where the train stopped. The Au Sable River in particular, gained the attention of fishermen and hunters as parties of sportsmen paddled up and down the stream in search of game. Stories in 1878 and 1879 in The Detroit Free Press and in Scribner's Monthly about deer hunting and fishing on the Au Sable and those wonderful Grayling Trout added immeasurably to the cachet of the area.

In the late 1870's it took about as long to reach Roscommon from Edna or Houghton Lake as it did to reach Roscommon from Bay City. The Michigan Central ran either one or two trains to Roscommon each day in addition to special excursions to Bay City or other locations. It was common for Roscommon residents to take a relaxing train ride for a one day or overnight excursion. But if you lived in Edna and needed to go to Roscommon for a day's business, you were in for a long, tiring day. You might take a horse and wagon or, if you were in a hurry, you would walk as the road from Edna to Roscommon was exceedingly bad. Depending upon the recent weather, the road might be impassable for a horse and buggy since a good part of the way was through a wet-lands area where the road dissolved into a muck-laden trail. Most times the road was bad and sometimes impassable, those with buggies had to make long detours to avoid getting stuck. The newspaper explained:

"Harvey Emory was known as a great walker and one day he was walking to Roscommon when he came upon a neighbor, Tom Knight, also on his way to Roscommon with a team and wagon. Tom said, 'Hop on and ride, Harvey.' Harvey replied, ' Can't do it, I'm in a hurry.'

Harvey went on his way, did his business in Roscommon, ate lunch and was walking home when he met Tom and his wagon still on his way to Roscommon."

The road between Houghton Lake and Roscommon remained an unimproved dirt, sand and muck trail for several years until lumber companies improved the road by creating a corduroy road through the wet areas. These 'logways' were created by laying down six inch diameter logs, side by side, then covering them with brush and smaller poles before coating the entire assemblage with a layer of soil. The 'logways' made a passable road when it was new but it soon became a bumpy, washboard surface when the dirt washed away in the spring rains and left the logs exposed. It wasn't until the road surface was built up with thick layers of gravel (and then asphalt in more recent times) that the road became a smooth, comfortable passageway.

In those early days roads were maintained by men who lived nearby. The county had no money for professional road maintenance and so a system was established whereby residents were periodically assigned a section of road to maintain. The system didn't work very well. Most of the men who were assigned road maintenance didn't have the tools, talents, or interest to maintain the roads. The result was that travelers suffered from no signs, bumps, holes, mud, fallen trees, confusing short-cuts, an occasional tree stump, and other impediments.

The road maintenance program was so bad that travelers often stopped before going on a road to inquire at a farm house about road maintenance. If the owner answered, 'why yes, Joe So-and-So recently had his team of horses out to work on the road' - most travelers would retrace their steps to find another road that hadn't been recently cared-for so they could continue their journey with some confidence.

Edna, Houghton Lake, St. Helen and the former Roscommon Station which became Roscommon, were the primary villages of the county in the late 1870's. The men and women who laid claim to the land and lived there totaled only several hundred people; however, the real estate market began heating up as lumbermen began buying large chunks of Roscommon County land for logging. James Harcourt, George Robinson, Charles Lyons and other Roscommon business men, including at least one saloon owner, John Mahoney, kept themselves busy in arranging deals for Roscommon land.

Peter Pruden saw the same opportunities as James Harcourt around Houghton Lake and he soon built a large structure that he called Pruden House. The building was a hotel, saloon, and restaurant built to satisfy the Saturday night celebrations of lumberjacks and their bosses, those traveling lumbermen who came and went as they checked on the status of their investments. The Pruden Hotel, a large two story frame building with a plain exterior, became a favorite of locals as they enjoyed the restaurant and bar. Pruden was an effective business man as he included among his guests both locals and tourists who came to fish and enjoy the bounty of Houghton Lake.

Like Houghton Lake, tourism at Higgins Lake in the latter part of the 1870's continued to grow as more and more campers came and spent a part or all of their summer at the lake. The first camper was Lorenzo Burrows and he introduced many of his fellow Saginaw residents to the lake including his brother, George Burrows. After Burrows and friends first camped in tents, they decided to build small cabins to make their summer excursions to the lake more comfortable. Burrows arranged for George Cheney to deliver lumber to the campsite, (from Cheney's saw mill) and a number of tiny cabins were built that were rented to vacationers who were mostly Saginaw residents and friends of Burrows.

Lorenzo and his wife managed the camp by providing food that was served at a community kitchen for each cabin. After a few years of renting, Lorenzo decided to begin selling lots along the lakeshore for permanent houses and the resort community known as Lakeside began.

George Burrows, Founder of Lakeside

In short order Lakeside was followed by two similar communities of campers along the lake. These two were Pinewood (mostly campers from Bay City) and Cottage Grove (started by campers from the Burrows camp). The increasing volume of campers to the lake added to the business at Roscommon and Cheney as each supplied goods and services for the campers. One of the continuing services provided was the transportation of campers from the railroad station to the lake.

One of the Original Modest Two-Family Burrow's Cabins

During the boom years of the logging era, Roscommon developed an unsavory reputation as a purveyor of sin for the lumberjacks. Accordingly, many of the families from Saginaw who vacationed at Higgins wanted to avoid Roscommon Station in fear of encounters with the shanty boys. For a while, these proper folks made it a point to ride the train past Roscommon to Cheney and then hire Mr. Cheney's team and wagon for a trip to the lake.

The fear of the shanty boys was short-lived. Soon the vacationers were employing teams and wagons from Roscommon for the trip to the lake. The operator that handled the most traffic to the lake in the 1880's was the Roscommon businessman, Chas. Blanchard. The hard-working, young Mr. Blanchard was engaged in several businesses in Roscommon including buying, selling and stabling horses. Thus, a natural outgrowth of his stable business was the organizing and managing of a stage coach line from the railroad station to Higgins Lake. By the late 1880's the traffic to the lake was sufficiently high that he was running two stages per day to the lake.

Lakeside Children with the Roscommon Stage

The naming of Roscommon Station as the county seat in 1879 provided the village a boost like a shot of adrenalin. Several men who sought to profit from county business left Houghton Lake village and moved to Roscommon Station which began to be known simply as Roscommon. The attorney H. H. Woodruff and others involved in government business, including land sales, suddenly decided that Roscommon had more to offer than Houghton Lake. Even the newspaper that began its publication in 1876 in Houghton Lake, *The Roscommon County Pioneer,* gave up and a new paper, *The Roscommon News*, began publication in Roscommon.

While the vacationers were enjoying their summers at the lakes, lumbermen from all around Michigan were surveying Roscommon County's timber lands and planning camps and transportation routes for the cut logs. Even though the railroad was happy to supply transport for logs, the rates were too high for most lumbermen who relied on Michigan's rivers and streams for virtually free transport of logs to one of the large saw mills located at the coast. (The logs were delivered to the saw mills through the efforts of booming companies that charged nominal fees for shepherding the logs).

The earliest lumbermen concentrated their logging operations along the rivers where it was easiest to transport the cut logs by floating them to the mills during the spring-time flows of high water. After these easily accessible logs were cut, lumbermen moved on to the logs around the lakes and streams that flowed into the main river systems. Thus, active logging operations began at camps around Higgins Lake, The Cut River, Houghton Lake and smaller streams like Denton and Backus Creeks that led to the lakes.

The Backus brothers from East Saginaw, John and Gottfried, owned property along the Cut River and used that stream for logging. The logging company of A. W. Wright began establishing camps around Houghton Lake as did the newly formed Roscommon Lumber Co. One of Wright's associates was Thomas Nester, an Irish immigrant. He and Wright compared notes and each bought large tracts of timber land, Wright at Houghton Lake and Nester in the southeast of the county along the headwaters of the Shiawassee.

In 1874, Higgins Lake was unaffected by logging. One lady who camped there remembered seeing the lake at sunset completely ringed by trees in an unbroken vista of green forests reflected at the edge of the shivering water. By 1879 the ring had large gaps as lumbermen had taken much of the timber that was easily "put-in" the lake. The Burrows family and other owners of camps on the north part of the lake resisted the trend – they retained the virgin timber.

On the south shore of the lake, lumberman John Monet banked 3 million board feet in 1879 near the present site of the Lyons Township Hall. Soon thereafter, the forests all around the lake except for the north end were gone.

Stacking Logs Until Spring (Michelson collection)

Logs that were banked on Higgins Lake required several months to reach the saw mills at Muskegon. After the ice melted in the spring, the Higgins Lake logs would be corralled in a raft and floated to the Cut River where they would proceed downstream after the dam was opened to increase water flow. From there, the logs were sent to Houghton Lake where they were again rafted to the outlet of the Muskegon River where they spent months in making the long trip to the mill.

Of course, by the time the logs arrived at the mill they were all mixed up with thousands of logs from the many jobbers who cut and transported their logs in the same waters. The solution to getting paid for your logs was to have each log marked with an identifying mark that was exclusive to the owner of the log. Hence, the log mark was invented wherein each log was stamped with a sort of brand that was hammered in. The marks were approved, legally recognizable security marks that were registered at the county clerk's office at the log's origin. BY 1945, Roscommon County had a total of 145 registered marks for logs.

Around the village of Roscommon loggers began to cut timber along the streams that led to the Au Sable: the South Branch and Robinson Creek [another one of those Robinson namesakes].

The population of the village of Roscommon grew after it became the official county seat. In 1877 the State of Michigan Gazatteer listed its population as 100, by 1981 the number had become 600. The added businesses in 1879 were a new lumber manufacturer, J. Robbins and Co.(that supported local building), a new shoemaker, and two new saloons to support the growing liquor trade. On the other side of the ledger, Roscommon's first church, the First Congregation Church shepherded by Rev. E. Branch in 1875, built their first structure in 1877 to house the flock, a white frame building with an imposing steeple. As the next decade loomed, business prospects looked bright indeed. In fact, a boom was just about to occur.

152

Downtown Roscommon's Largest Buildings – The Opera House (right of photo) **and The Pioneer House** (left side beyond Ford sign)

Photo from Roscommon Centennial Publication

Chapter 10

Boom Times

In 1870 the population of Michigan was 1.2 million people. In a short 20 years, the population of the state nearly doubled to 2.1 million. In Roscommon County during the same period the population went from near zero to more than two thousand, a near infinite increase. Those who came were overwhelmingly young, and full of energy. A few of these were wealthy, anxious to expand their wealth. They came for a while and then left, moving somewhere else for further riches or more comforts. Those who were poorer came for a chance to earn a decent living. Many of them stayed, establishing roots to the communities and rearing families who are still here. In either case of rich or poor, it was the logging that brought them here.

While the lumbermen were establishing camps all around Roscommon County in the later part of the 1870's, settlers were creeping in as well. Most came to work in the lumber industry at the camps or to provide the many supplies needed for the camps. A few, like John and James Nolan, were young men who came to try their luck at farming in 1878. The Nolan's, numbered among the first permanent settlers in Richfield Township, hadn't far to come; their home was just across the county border to the south, a place called Nolan Station, a lumberman's home.

The Nolan brothers became stalwart citizens, providing the first white child born in the area, Bruce Nolan, 1885, and the first teacher, Carrie Nolan, and the first township supervisor, James. The township came into being in 1885 when the State Legislature decided to split off a new township from Higgins. At one of the first township meetings, it was decided to name the new township Richfield. The person suggesting the name was none other than the active James Nolan.

The lumber boom in Roscommon County was in full force by 1880 with camps scattered from north to south and east to west. Most of the camps were a stone's throw from one of the lakes or rivers. The Au Sable and Au Gres River valleys led the state in the number of board feet sent by river in 1880. In 1884, The Muskegon River led the state in the same statistic. Roscommon County was a key source for the logs that were sent down both river systems.

The camps and the shanty boys provided opportunities for other people to settle nearby and provide services the camps and their workers wanted and needed to operate. Horses in the camp needed feed, men needed food, and the camp needed tools. The shanty boys wanted recreation on Saturday nights when the work was done and the settlements near the camps were only too happy to supply what they wanted.

Settlements that existed for any length of time also wanted mail delivery from the post office and those records indicate the presence and location of many of Roscommon's ghost towns that existed because of the camps. The larger post offices were at the main villages of Edna, Roscommon, Houghton Lake and St. Helen but a number of other post offices were located at the small settlements next to the camps. At least 20 different settlements existed in the county during some part of the lumbering era. Here are those known to exist and their locations.

Achill…. in Nester Township near Achel Lake
Ackliss….in Roscommon Township, near Robinson Lake
Coy……… 8 miles east of Roscommon
Crooks….in Lake Township, near the Dead Stream
Geels…. see text, along old 76
Herbert….in Richfield Township, east of Roscommon
Keno…. see text, along old 76
Kirkland… in Denton Township on Denton Creek south of highway M 18
Loxley…. in Denton Township south of the State Police post

Lyon Manor.... see text, just south of Higgins Lake

Markey.... in Markey Township (named after real estate agent and politician D. P. Markey, the village had 3 saw mills and a population of 300 in 1917)

Michelson.... see text, west of Houghton Lake

Nellsville.... in Denton Township near the M 55 & State Police Post

Nolan.... in Nester Township near Nolan and Muma Road

Moore.... see text, along old 76

Moorestown.... in Lyon Township, west of Higgins Lake

Prices....in Higgins Township, 2 miles south of Roscommon west of M 18

Terney.... see text, along old 76

Verncroft....in Nester Township near Atchel and the county line

These numerous settlements were established as a direct result of the lumber trade. Most disappeared quickly when the camps moved on. Some held on for a number of years before they too disappeared. Now they exist only as memories or as abandoned relics mostly covered with forest growth. Only a few road signs mark their locations in acknowledgement of locations that once were homes for busy, active people.

In the 1880's, St. Helen was not the only village in Richfield Township on the east side of the county. Along the railroad line to the northwest of St. Helen another tiny village was situated, first called Hardscrabble and then changed to Geels in honor of the lumberman by that name and his nearby camp. Directly to the south of St. Helen a small farming village evolved, initially referred to as the Towner Settlement after its founder, Jay Towner. The Towner Settlement became Maple Valley some years later when a new store was built and identified as the Maple Valley Store for the nearby stand of maple trees.

Keno was the name chosen for another small farming village located six miles due north of St. Helen (along current road F 97). This village was named for a horse. One of the farmers in the area had a stable of fine horses and the best of the lot became well-known - so well known that people named a village in its honor!

The railroad between St. Helen and Roscommon traveled in a northwesterly direction, generally following the course of South Branch of the Au Sable. Lumbermen soon decided that it was a suitable stream for "putting in" and a number of camps were built between the two villages.

Ultimately, three settlements that each took the name of the nearby lumbering camp grew up; Geels, Terney and Moore. The railroad wanted to take advantage of the freight business at each and a siding was added at each settlement approximately 2, 5, and 8 miles from St Helen.

Geels Road and Moore Road intersect just west of old 76 near the site of the two former settlements

Lonely Geels Road Sign Recalls Site of Former Settlement

Lumbering around Houghton and Higgins Lakes soon consumed all the timber close to the lakes using short logging roads to 'put-in' the logs. After these areas were logged, the lumbermen were forced to transport the logs further and further to the water on sleds over iced roads. As the technology improved, big wheels helped in the movement of logs from the cutting areas to the roads and the areas where the logs were skidded before the spring drives.

As time wore on, W. S. Gerrish demonstrated the value of small gage railroad trains and the technology quickly spread to Roscommon. Suddenly, logging and movement of logs could be done in warmer weather further from the lakes. The camps belonging to A. W, Wright Lumbering, The Roscommon Lumber Co. John Murray, and Blodgett and Byrne were cutting timber in all directions around the lakes. On the east side of Higgins Lake another Jobber operating a lumber camp was Abner H. Gerrish. Abner was the brother of the famous logger Winfield Scott Gerrish who had developed the practice of using narrow gage railroads for logging. Another brother, Joseph Gerrish, served as the clerk in Abner's camp. Both brothers worked in Roscommon for a period but claimed their residence in Clare County.

Enough residents lived in the area and around the Gerrish camp in 1880 to justify a separate legislative township for them. They hadn't lived there long, however, as evidenced by the fact that the first babies born to settlers were the twins Alice and Mabel Marsh born in 1879. In fact, there were just 215 people in Gerrish on June 6, 1880 – 198 men and 17 women.

 Residents of the surrounding area used the Gerrish camp for a meeting that is now commemorated with a Michigan Historical Marker.

"Near this site on April 5, 1880, area residents met at the Gerrish Logging Camp to elect officers for their newly formed township. James Watson was chosen as the first supervisor. Originally the township embraced present-day Gerrish, Lyon and Markey townships…." (Markey was split off from Gerrish in 1887).

Generally the immigrants to Roscommon County were families or single men who came to work in the camps. Consequently there were always considerably more single men than single women of marriageable age. One female who arrived as a single lady in the county was Miss Prudence Doonan.

Miss Doonan came with her father, John Doonan, to Roscommon in 1882. Her father was employed as foreman in running a lumbering camp and he brought along his eldest daughter to serve as a cook in camp. Her stay in Roscommon was intended to be temporary, only until the foreman's job at the camp had ended. Things didn't quite work out that way as the young lady met and then married a Roscommonite in 1884, one Mr. Charles Lyons. Charles and Prudence (most folks called her Dotty) decided to take advantage of the business boom in Roscommon and so the two agreed to manage a hotel in the bustling little lumber town. The Northern, it was called. Business in the hotel was good and the two lovebirds managed the operation for 14 years, with Dotty supervising the cooking. As things slowed down in the latter part of the decade, the two decided that better things were in store for them if only they owned a farm.

The Northern Hotel in Downtown Roscommon (Hotel Burned Down in 1918)

Finally they found property to their liking near the shore of Higgins Lake and so they bought land for. Their farm had a distinct advantage over others; it was on the southwest shore of the beautiful lake and it seemed to beckon tourists. Almost as soon as they got established they noticed the tourists coming for visits and their farm was like a magnet. Soon they returned to their old business but at a new address; they opened a summer hotel at the farm to serve those who came to the lake to enjoy the fishing, cool breezes, and all the lake had to offer for the summer season. Lyons Manor, they called it, and soon other resorts and other businesses became established nearby, aided by the real estate development efforts of Charles. Mapmakers began naming the settlement after the hotel -Lyon Manor. After a while, the settlement lent its name to local government and the resulting township became known as Lyons.

By the accounts of the time, the former Miss Prudence Doonan had a successful life as wife, helpmeet and mother. Sadness struck the family early when her son became ill with pneumonia and died suddenly. Prudence attended his funeral and, overcome with grief, she too fell ill, having caught a cold during the funeral services. Prudence's illness took command and the medicine of time was not equal to the task. One week later, she was dead at age 49.

As the population swelled and new legislative townships were defined, other political changes occurred as well. During the election of 1886, Peter Pruden opposed the re-election of Albert Denton as Supervisor of Denton Township. When the vote was counted Denton had won but only by a single vote. Pruden demanded a recount and it was determined that he had won the election due to an illegal vote for Denton. An angry Denton packed up and moved away and so a new postmaster was needed to replace Edna. Pruden was named postmaster and he promptly changed the location of the post office to his hotel. Soon, his name was being used for the post office and the village surrounding it. The name stuck. Prudenville has endured for past 125 years in testimony of Pruden's election and business acumen.

Even though the *Roscommon News* focused mostly on news from the village of Roscommon, in May, 1886, the editor ran a piece concerning the newly-named Prudenville.

May 28, 1886

The News visits Houghton Lake -"The first place met is the thriving little village of Prudenville located along Denton Creek on the shore of Houghton Lake. It contains two stores, a post office, blacksmith shop, two hotels, a first-class sawmill, shoe shop, two saloons, and is the terminus of the C. B. Field logging [rail] road which runs right through the village and some distance into the lake on a trestle work roadway. This road is a feature of the village and will no doubt be highly beneficial as it will shortly give access and ingress, the citizens think, by running excursion trains and they sincerely hope, a mail train daily. Trains of some 15 cars loaded with logs come in every two hours and the unloaders, who are stationed at the entrance to the trestle works, quickly knock loose the binding chains and board the cars [and] when they reach clear water the ten or twelve men stationed there send the logs flying from both sides of the cars to the water. It is rather dangerous work but comparatively few accidents happen.

"At the Pruden House, a large and pleasing structure, business was found flourishing under the genial manager's care who extended every cordiality and hospitality, and on visiting the store of P. W. Pruden, proprietor of the hotel, that hearty gentleman was found, and he was quite anxious to promote the town. He has a commodious store and good stock and devotes his time principally to his duties there.

Dresden Bryan is replacing the mill (owned by Pruden) that burned some time ago and it is nearly ready for business. He intends it to be one of the most complete of its kind and it will manufacture for a building in the wood line; shingles, lath flooring, siding, sheeting and timber.

R. E. Titus has a well-equipped blacksmith shop in which he was at work on as fine a buggy as one would wish for in this part of the country. ..... A VISIT

TO THE MOUNDS FROM WHICH PREHISTORIC BONES HAVE BEEN TAKEN, (A SAMPLE OF WHICH MAY BE SEEN AT THIS OFFICE)...."

As the outlying villages grew with the boom in the lumber business, so did the village of Roscommon. Its designation as County Seat with its new court house attracted visiting lumbermen as they did their business with the county clerk. One of the required businesses that all participated in was the registering of the log marks they used on their logs before entrusting them to the lakes and rivers. The number of lumbermen in Roscommon is indicated by the number of registered log marks, 157 with the last being registered in 1945.

Roscommon's new court house was followed in short order with a new jail. The two frame buildings were each painted white and they both stood proudly on the crest of a small hill back from the street on the land donated by the wily George Robinson. At the beginning of the Roscommon boom times, Robinson felt that his real estate business was secure and so he contracted with a local man, J. O. Dildine, to take over sales of his Roscommon lands. George and his wife Helen moved back to Detroit and his law firm to continue working with his partner David Brooks. Robinson didn't stay away long as he was a frequent visitor making regular trips to Roscommon to consult with Dildine and sign legal documents.

Dildine was a good choice. He was a man well-known in Roscommon due to his many business ventures. He served as the only undertaker, he sold furniture, and he operated another business as a collections agent for past due bills. Sometime later he even strung copper wire for the new-fangaled invention known as a telephone. Selling Robinson land was just one more of his many undertakings as he ambled about town and made it a point to know what was happening in the village.

The First Congregational Church in 1880

New stores in the village began opening in rapid succession. Edward Kiely's general store specialized in supplying lumber camps and his business blossomed. By 1881 the town boasted of 3 churches, a school, 6 hotels, J. Robbin's steam sawmill, several stores, 2 doctors, 4 lawyers, Bartholomew's drugstore, 2 barbers, a banker ,a meat market, furniture store, a blacksmith, hardware store, billiard hall, and clothing store. The shoemaker also made boots and advertised his boots for use by 'river hogs – A. .J Mc Gillis, bootmaker'. The hotels included on-premises saloons offering beer and liquor. The town had changed from a northern outpost of the county to a 'full-service' supplier of whatever the residents needed. The population of the village of Roscommon had jumped six-fold in four years: from 100 in 1877 to 600 in 1881.

In addition to the businesses listed, the town also sported a newspaper, in fact, two newspapers for a five year period (see chapter 11 for more details). The area's first paper, *The Roscommon County Pioneer,* published by Amedius Zahn, moved to Roscommon from Houghton Lake in 1880. *The Pioneer* then competed with *The Roscommon News,* a Roscommon village paper published by Robert Ward. Ultimately, *The Roscommon Herald* succeeded the earlier papers.

The Roscommon Herald Newspaper Office

The principal business leaders in town began to worry about their enterprises and what would become of things if growth continued and no one had any say about how things were arranged. Sentiments of this nature led to discussions about forming a village council to manage things. In 1882 Roscommon became incorporated as a village with an official Board of Supervisors. The businessmen saw to it that some of their own were elected: the first business owner in 1875 Dan Bennett was elected President of the Board with trustees, Eugene Kiely (general store and supplier of the camps) Geo. Alexander (store owner), and H. H. Woodruff (attorney). The other officers were City Clerk J. O. Dildine and Treasurer W. B. Orcutt (a banker).

The Roscommon boom continued in 1883 as the population climbed to 800 people and more new businesses were established: a seller of books and notions, a dentist, dressmaker, baker, wagon maker, milliner, real estate surveyor, architect, photographer, machinist, and music teacher. Not listed in any of the official business listings but known to all the shanty boys far and wide were also saloons/bawdy houses. One of the best known saloons, The Occidental, was owned by a young man, a former lumberjack by the name of John Mahoney. Mahoney was also listed as a lumber manufacturer and dealer in pine lands but in fact he spent most of this time and energy in the saloon. He told the 1880 census taker that his profession was a 'saloonist'. He didn't explain about the four unmarried females living in this house at the time who listed their occupation as 'servants' but all the shanty boys who lined up at his place on Saturday nights knew exactly what services they could expect from the servants. Mahoney's early partner was a man named Danny Dunn who made such a name for himself in the sin business that he is discussed in a following chapter.

One of the new things in Roscommon in 1883 was an Opera House. Every self-respecting town had an Opera House in those days and Roscommon residents weren't to be denied the pleasures of entertainment that could be had a community's Opera House. So it was in the early part of 1883 that a group of influential citizens came together and decided to get the ball rolling. They set up a business organization, The Opera House Company, with a Board of Directors and stockholders to raise the necessary cash for a new building. The two story building was built on the corner of Lake and

Main and the proud Directors, Dan Bennett, E. W. Grant and Tom Macklin welcomed everyone at its first opening.

The Opera House was a multi-purpose building with the main auditorium on the second floor and a store for rent on the first floor along with some business offices. The idea for the store and offices was that those spaces would be rented to derive regular income from the property. The venture was a rousing success. The available space was soon rented and the auditorium soon was in demand for many civic events as well as a site for shows by traveling acts.

The Opera House soon became an essential part of village life. The first High School graduation ceremony was held there, the Village Council held their regular meetings there and the public library used space on the first floor. The Opera House became the center of activities for many in the village.

First High School Graduation is Held in the Opera House

The very first Roscommon graduates were all females and all were familiar names to Roscommon folks: Verna Blanchard, Alice Kiely, Frances Baldwin, Rena Griffin and Adelia McCrea

Things looked rosy in the village of Roscommon and throughout Roscommon County in 1883. The lumber business was growing and was active throughout the county as attested to by the scores of small settlements that dotted the entire county. The four major villages, Edna, Houghton Lake, St. Helen and Roscommon, each served as the center of economic activity for their area as lumbermen bought and sold in their fevered pursuit of profits from the 'green gold' – the seeming unending supply of logs for lumber.

The village of Roscommon developed into the largest of the four and had more business than the other villages as result of its status as County Seat. Residents from all over the county regularly visited the village. It was such a central part of life for shopping, entertainment and business of various sorts that people who spoke of 'Roscommon', invariably referred to the village, not the county. The village had a darker side as well. Each of the shanty boys who visited Roscommon knew all about that side as they frequently visited to take advantage of what the village offered as men like Danny Dunn and John Mahoney practiced their trade of separating men from their money.

Chapter 11

Roscommon's Underbelly

In 1880 the village of Roscommon became a boom town along with the rest of the county. The boom times were stimulated by the lumber trade and the village served the various interests of that trade: the camps that needed provisions for men and animals and the owners and managers who needed legal and financial services as well as accommodations during their visits. The other important economic impact came with the shanty boys themselves whenever they came to town, mostly on weekends or whenever the camps shut down.

The shanty boys or 'jacks,' as they were often called, came to town looking for relief from the hard, dangerous, drudgery of life in the woods bent over a saw or an axe or a chain that was coupled to a heavy, balky log. The work was hard, often dangerous, and mostly tedious. Many of the jacks were young and they sought the pleasures of alcohol, women and gambling in town, all of which were prohibited at the camp. Camp rules were strict; any violations meant you were out of a job. The townsfolk who traded in such things were only too happy to provide what was wanted, at exorbitant prices, of course.

Like other boom towns, Roscommon developed a reputation for its services in the sin business. Whether or not the reputation was deserved is a question that is debatable then and now. In an 1886 edition, The *Roscommon News* complained about a story being unfair that was reported in another newspaper about Roscommon's unsavory character. Yet, it is to be noted that some Higgins Lake residents refused to leave the train at the Roscommon Station because of the rowdy behavior of visiting jacks. One author reported that Roscommon was awash in saloons during its boom times, reporting a count of 20 to 22 saloons during them mid 1880's. The historical record in the newspaper suggests otherwise: the County Treasurer reported that income for 1886 included the selling of (*only*) 14 liquor licenses for the county. A separate accounting in 1883 by another observer listed 12 establishments in the village of Roscommon that are believed to have been either a saloon or an establishment (like a hotel) that included the selling of whiskey. In another undated accounting of 33 buildings in the village, 11 were saloons. So it is a little unclear exactly how many saloons there were. Let's just say there were more than 10, a lot for a small village with a few hundred souls.

By the standards of the 21st century, these numbers seem like an extraordinary dedication to drinking alcohol. Yet, if you visit a place today where the population has a very high percentage of young men, like the Navy town of Norfolk, Virginia, the percentage of saloons in Roscommon in the 1880's seems a little less overwhelming. Roscommon's count doesn't seem so extraordinary compared to other boom towns like Seney, Mi. with its 21 saloons. (see the following story of Seney and Dan Dunn) The champion in this event of saloon keeping must have been the small town of Hurley, Wisconsin, just across the border from Michigan's Ironwood in the Upper Peninsula. There, a boom from iron mining occurred during the end of lumbering in Roscommon. Hurley grew in one year from practically zero to the status of boom town. The one year old town boasted 2 churches, 2 Opera houses, 15 stores, no jails and **40 saloons.**

Roscommon developed a reputation among lumberjacks and others of being a wide open town compared to Grayling and nearby lumbering towns. One story from Bert Harcourt, perhaps an exaggeration, recalls a lumberjack's trip on the Michigan Central train from Bay City. The jack got on the train drunk with no ticket. The conductor asked the young man where he was headed. "To Hell, I suppose" he managed to utter. The Conductor thereupon made out a ticket for him to Roscommon.

Roscommon may have gotten off to a bad footing with one of its first business persons, a Frenchwoman from Canada who had seen her share of life. Ursule Mercier got off the train in 1872 shortly after the station had opened at the remote spot. The dark haired, stocky 33 year old woman with the dark complexion somehow managed to appropriate an empty boxcar at the station. She established a temporary saloon and gambling establishment in the boxcar, using one end to serve liquor and the other to maintain a table for gambling. Ursule seemed undaunted by the rough shanty boys who came her way as she served as owner, barmaid and bouncer for the makeshift establishment. It was said that if a fight broke out, Ursule was in it. Within a few months she had earned enough to begin construction on one of the first hotels in the village, one that featured a full service saloon, of course.

By 1880 the 41 year old Ursule had her family with her and she told the census taker that she was N. Celina Mercier (she was often called Mrs. Mercer by local residents), that she lived in Higgins Township, was married to a 33 year old laborer named William Mercier and that she ran a hotel, otherwise known as the Pioneer House and now called the Spruce Motor Lodge.

Two other capable and tough women ran saloons in Roscommon during the lumbering era. One was Mrs. James Raizon, operator of a place in 1883 that was listed as The Raizon Saloon and at other times known as The Roscommon House. The Gordon house was another drinking and sleeping establishment that was run by Mrs. Gordon, known to all as a kind, gentle woman who tried to run a nice place. Mrs. Gordon's courage came to be admired in the aftermath of a fight that broke out between Jim Farley and a man named McGillen. Farley got the better of McGillen by using a razor that resulted in McGillen's blood spewing everywhere. Aid for McGillen was hampered when two men fainted while trying to assist. There was nothing for it until Mrs. Gordon stepped up and took over the job and then calmly cleaned up the spilt blood.

The boom town feel came to Roscommon County and the village of Roscommon after the lumbering business became white hot in 1880. The boom continued for five years and then began to fade as the forests all around the area were consumed. The shanty boys who came to town when the camps weren't working kept the local business men and a few county officers on their toes in keeping order.

A correspondent in 1882 records his observations for March 6 just prior to an election. *"There is considerable excitement here over the village election to take place tomorrow. The town is full of the harder-looking lot of woodsmen we have ever seen congregated and fighting and drunkenness is the rule rather than the exception as is shown by the fact that while walking around one block I counted 17 men carrying evidence of hard-fought battles in the shape of black eyes, bandaged heads, chawed up fingers, toes, ears, etc. A fracas occurred Saturday night between two saloon men in which one of them was terribly punished. While this melee was in progress, a horse doctor drew a revolver and fired out the window and shot a man for himself, the ball inflicting only a slight wound in the arm. "*

Roscommon's Sherriff and Prosecutor kept busy during the times the camps weren't working in keeping the shanty boys in line. The Prosecutor's report for 1885 indicated the following legal actions;

Complaint	Number of Cases
Assualt & Battery	9
Disorderly	1
Indecent exposure	3
Keeping a house of ill fame	1
Larceny	2
Illegal voting	7
Printing indecent literature	1
Search Warrant	1
Vagrancy	1
Drunkenness	34

Drunkenness was a particular problem for lumberjacks. Some stories about the jacks and their drinking were funny while others were sad. The following has elements of each.

The Roscommon News, March 19, 1886:

"Joseph Lagner of Bay City entered a saloon Friday night and, while the owner was engaged elsewhere, inserted a rubber hose into the bung hole of a barrel of liquor and drank a large quantity. He left the saloon but fell in the street. He was found insensible at 10:00. He lingered until 1:00 Saturday when he died."

Drinking was a problem not only for the visiting lumberjacks but also for some of the townsfolk. One of the town's businesses was a drug store that was owned and operated by an Indian known as 'Old Kenwendeshon'. In addition to his drug store, Kenwendeshon billed himself as a physician and surgeon. The story is told of him that he once got a barrel of "squirrel whiskey" that he sampled. He was so proud of his whiskey that he invited a Roscommon bartender, Bert Hess, to come for a look and a taste. The sampling of the whiskey went a little too far and Kenwendeshon became totally inebriated and decided it would be entertaining to bowl over a stack of drug bottles in his store. Soon he was throwing bottles around, including one that went through the front plate glass window of his store.

Undeterred, the Indian decided to pursue further entertainment at a nearby saloon, the Occidental. Once there he found his way to the dining area and pounced on a catsup bottle that he used to effect in splashing the ceiling and walls. By this time the bartender at the Occidental caught up with the Indian and chased him into the street, the Indian running at full speed with his coattail flying behind him. He wasn't seen around town for some while.

Alcohol was a problem throughout much of the state during this period and a political movement was initiated to ban the sale of all alcohol. The movement had some success and by late 1886 and a bill was introduced in the Michigan legislature to ban alcohol sales completely. After much debate and hand wringing the bill was voted upon in April 1887 and rejected by the state legislature to the relief of many in the booming areas.

Carry Amelia Moore Nation

Carry Nation, Famous Prohibitionist of the 1880's

The most notorious of those in the sin business in Roscommon was Danny Dunn. Danny was born in Detroit about 1853 and grew up there in a large family. As soon as he was able to make it on his own, he left home to become a lumberjack, slowly making his way north to the camps around Saginaw. He ended up at Camp 16 along the Tittabawassee River, home to any number of tough shanty boys. Dunn seemed to fit right in with the brawling, fighting, hard-drinking bunch and he counted as his friends those who liked to drink and party as much as he did.

Other than being a red-haired, hot tempered jack, not too much is known of his youth other than his heritage, Irish, and that made him a fairly common citizen of the north woods. Dunn apparently spent enough time as a jack so that he knew the appetites of those who spent most of their time at the end of a saw or an axe, and the rest of their time in a saloon. Danny was like many other jacks, ready for a barroom fight just for the fun of it, although Danny was a little different than some of the other fighters since he knew when to run if things didn't go in his favor.

The most famous tough jack in a country full of them was Silver Jack Driscoll. Silver Jack was known far and wide as a fighter and no one had ever seen him take a beating from any other jack. Dunn didn't have the reputation of Silver Jack, but he liked to fight and he may have been looking for a chance to improve his standing in the camps as a fighting tough. As luck would have it, Danny and Silver Jack ended up in the same saloon one night when Danny seemed to be spoiling for a fight. He challenged the bigger man, Silver Jack, in a mistaken show of bravado. Danny had miscalculated. The tough Silver Jack was soon making short shrift of Dunn and it looked like he was beyond hope when suddenly he pulled a knife, a cowardly act given the barroom rules of no weapons beyond your calked boots and fingers that were sufficient for stomping faces and gouging eyes. As Silver Jack stepped back to reassess the situation, Danny showed his colors by running for the door, not to be seen again that night.

Thus armed with the knowledge that there were some men that he couldn't handle with his fists, Danny ended his career in the woods at Camp 16, one of the many camps in the Saginaw Valley along the Tittabawassee River, just south of Roscommon County.

Dunn drifted into Bay City where he went to work in a saloon acting as a bouncer. The job didn't last too long as it became apparent that even though Dunn was a big man at six feet tall and 220 pounds, he was knocked out by a smaller, tougher man. Dunn then hooked up with another former jack and tough, John Mahoney, and the two decided they could earn more money by selling whiskey than by drinking it. Dunn started out as a bartender working for Mahoney and the two soon became partners. The partnership didn't last. Mahoney had four young women as prostitutes for his business and Dunn was struck with one girl in particular, Sadie Love. Sadie was a hired by Mahoney and lived in his house but Dunn evidently wasn't prejudiced by her profession as he soon proposed marriage to her. Sadie agreed to his proposal and the two were united in matrimony.

Mahoney had started his Roscommon business sometime before 1880. He told the 1880 census clerk his occupation was 'saloonist.' He noted that he was single but he didn't explain about the four young women who lived in his house. Mahoney was 24 years old at the time and the girls were Sarah Love (Sadie), age 22, Mary Thompson, 24, Lucy Spencer, 25, and sadly, another Love who was likely Sadie's younger sister, Belle Love, age 18 (at home amongst her family, Belle was known as Isabel Love). Each of the young women told the census clerk that she was a servant. Like Dunn, Mahoney gave his heritage as Irish.

Sadie evidently harbored sentimental feelings for her former employer even though she married Dunn, as she didn't object to an occasional romp in bed with the aforementioned Mahoney. Dunn must have been somewhat suspicious of Sadie's trip to Bay City that coincided with Mahoney's trip and so Dunn followed the pair and discovered the two in bed. A divorce followed and Mahoney and Dunn got in a fight, ending their partnership.

Before Dunn and Mahoney split up, the two were partners in a bar they called the Occidental Hotel and Saloon. The saloon part of the Occidental was a large barroom and dining room with swinging double doors and a bar that was divided in half.

Mahoney was involved in several businesses, he called himself a dealer in pine lands and he worked as a jobber in cutting lumber. Mahoney was considerable smaller than Dunn and some of the lumberjacks, but he kept order by means of a revolver that he always carried. Dunn favored a knife that he was known to pull out at the least provocation.

Mahoney left Roscommon before 1886 to pursue opportunity in another growing town in another remote area; along the shore of Lake Superior where iron mining was stimulating the growth of a boom town. The Roscommon News noted the event on Oct. 29, 1886: "John Mahoney,

formerly of Roscommon, has a fine hotel in Ashland (Wisconsin)" Given
Mahoney's past, his hotel in Ashland was probably the same sort of
business in satisfying men's baser desires as he had done in Roscommon.
Like Dunn, Mahoney seemed partial to Sadie and so the two became one
and the amorous Sadie became Mrs. Mahoney. The Mahoney's story is a
sad one. Just two years after the Roscommon News report about his fine
'hotel', Mahoney died - murdered, some say, at age 33, and was buried in
Ashland County, Wisconsin. Sadie lasted only another two years before she
followed her husband in death. She was also buried in the Ashland Mount
Hope cemetery after her death in 1890 at age 32.

Dunn had come to Roscommon County by 1878 and he had opened his
saloon and whorehouse at the populous area along the south side of
Houghton Lake. Dunn modeled his operation after others he had seen, and
there were plenty to look at as several villages that were close to lumber
camps had joints that Danny studied from the inside as well as outside.
Dunn's operation quickly became a roaring success to his thinking. Despite
the occasional brush with the law and the indignation of some God-fearing
local residents who tried unsuccessfully to close his operations, the
business was a money-maker. It attracted the usual collection of drunken,
rowdy types that most neighbors weren't too fond to see on their way to
church or when they went shopping. After a while the respectable ladies of
Houghton Lake and Prudenville decided that enough was enough and they
decided to take matters into their own hands. The result was that Dunn's
first establishment mysteriously caught fire.

Danny had a new building constructed and barely missed a beat. (Dunn
owned property near the current M55/M18 intersection highways where
the stone building now stands in Prudenville) But the respectable men and
women of southern Roscommon County weren't finished yet as another
fire broke out at his establishment. By this time things were hopping in the
village of Roscommon just as Dunn decided to seek greener pastures. He
decided to begin business in Roscommon where the jacks were just as
plentiful and the local officials were perhaps a bit more forgiving of a

business like his. Some called his new business Dunn's Bull Pen and there was no mistaking the services that he offered.

Dunn operated his Roscommon operation after similar establishments in Prudenville and Houghton Lake. In addition to his business with Mahoney at the Occidental Hotel and Saloon, Dunn opened a "ranch" across the South Branch just outside the village. The lumberjacks knew it as "Canaday" and he had no shortage of business when the jacks were in town. Since he felt he knew how to entertain men and separate them from their money, he also invested in another entertainment business, a pool hall that catered to mill workers and jacks in East Tawas at the mouth of the Au Sable River. It was there that Danny's temper got the best of him and he ended up in a bar fight where one man was killed. The law intervened and tracked Dunn to a nearby bar where he was drinking with little regard for the fight he had just been involved in. The result was that Dunn was sentenced to 18 months in state prison.

Dunn's problems continued after he left prison and returned to his saloon and whorehouse business. A competitor, one James Carr, a notorious saloon keeper and pimp who owned brothels in Meredith and Harrison just south of Roscommon, accused Dunn of arson in the burning of a saloon. Charges and counter charges were filed and some believed that both Carr and Dunn tried arson as the means to reduce competitive pressures. Dunn decided to leave Roscommon for greener pastures after he learned about the newest, rip-roaring lumber town in the Upper Peninsula; Seney, Michigan, known to some (including the post office) as "Helltown, USA." Again the newspaper reported the news: "On March 20, 1884, Danny Dunn closed his saloon and moved to Seney."

Seney developed quite a reputation among lumberjacks for gambling, corruption and even slavery (never proved). Seney hosted 21 saloons, 10 hotels, and one church. Some of the jacks called the place "Ram's Pasture" and behaved as if it were. Drinking, fighting, gambling and whoring were the expected pursuits for the shanty boys who came to town to relax and spend their money. Among those who called Seney their home during the lumbering era were the colorful characters named "Stub Foot O'Donnell," "Frying Pan" Mag and "Pump Handle" Joe.

Fights between the jacks were a common occurrence on Saturday nights. The saloon owners and other business men tolerated the fights with the attitude that the 'boys were just letting off a little steam." One of the epic fist fights occurred between "Wild Hughie" Logan and "Killer" Shea. In this battle ears were bitten and eyes gouged but it was a draw in the end. Not all the fights ended in such a convenient fashion however, and the town quickly developed a cemetery for jacks who had no known family – Boot Hill, they called it, and they sited it just south of town so no one had to interrupt their drinking for very long in attending to a burial. The nature of the men and the cemetery is suggested by one of the headstones which has a short inscription, **Died Fighten'**.

Before he left Roscommon, Dunn arranged to have his Roscommon bar/brothel burned in hopes of obtaining insurance proceeds. The case was finally adjudicated in December, 1885 in Detroit court. The Roscommon News reported this brief item: *"Dr. Washington was summoned to Detroit to appear as a witness in the insurance case of Daniel Dunn vs. Western Insurance Co. The case was terminated in the favor of the insurance company when Mr. Dunn didn't appear in court."*- Dec. 4, 1885

Dunn began in Seney where he had left off in Roscommon; he bought a building and started a saloon in town and opened a large, commodious brothel at the edge of town to satisfy the hard-drinking lumberjacks and also quench their thirsts of a different kind. As a kind of insurance, Dunn hired the toughest man he knew to keep order in the bar, his old nemesis, Silver Jack Driscoll. The business prospered immediately as the local lumber camps provided a supply of men who were just as anxious as those around Roscommon and Houghton Lake for the pleasures Dunn was offering. Then, almost immediately a problem developed. The man that Danny had hired to torch his building in Roscommon suddenly appeared in Seney and demanded money. It was blackmail. Nothing was ever proved but the man was never seen alive again after he visited Dunn.

Shortly after this, another man, this one a druggist, visited Dunn and asked when he should expect payment for the loan that was due that Dunn had borrowed some time before to start his Seney business. He too, was never heard from again. (The bones of the men were discovered some years later in a remote spot near Seney and it was widely accepted that Dunn had lured the men to the lonely spot and murdered each of them.)

Danny was never shy. He frequently visited Roscommon to check on his remaining business affairs and he regularly stopped in at the Roscommon News either for business or to report on his comings and goings as the following news items attest; *Oct. 30, 1885* – "Dan Dunn of Seney was in the village today." *Nov. 15, 1885*- "Dan Dunn of Seney was in the village this week." *March 20, 1884* –" Danny Dunn closed his saloon and moved to Seney".*Jan. 22, 1886* "Danny Dunn was in the village today" *April 2,1886*. Danny Dunn of Seney has sold his (business) interest to his partner, Nivins."(In an account from another source, Jack Nevins was listed as owning a bowling alley and saloon.)

Dunn was just one more of Seney's proprietors - the town had 21 saloons and at least two large whorehouses, as well as a number of prostitutes who operated independently. In a twist of fate, the ownership of the other whorehouse was a group well known to Dunn. The establishment was owned and operated by the Harcourt family, a group of six brothers who had grown up in the small village of Edna/Prudenville where most everyone knew everyone else and certainly everyone knew the infamous Dunn. (The patriarch of the Harcourt family owned the Harcourt Hotel in Prudenville)

The Harcourt's saw Dunn's entrance in the Seney business as an intrusion on their private fiefdom. Furthermore, Dunn's habit of dressing as a proper Victorian gentleman and his newfound abstinence from drinking, gambling and swearing galled them. Dunn had even gotten married to a lady and the two had sired a boy, Daniel, who died at age 11 months in Aug. 1886. It wasn't as if Danny had suddenly developed into a gentlemen, rather, it was more a realization that to remain in business and remain profitable required a certain appearance and a certain relationship with the political powers in the county.

Dunn Followed the Fashions of the Day like this 1880's Englishman Pictured in Life Magazine

Dunn made it a point to become a supporter of the local sheriff, never failing any opportunity to provide his support in a tangible manner in case he ran afoul of the law. His political maneuverings paid off; in 1888 he was charged with running a whorehouse but exonerated when no witnesses could be found despite the fact that the entire town knew of his business.

The Dunn/Harcourt feud intensified with Dunn's continued success. Finally, it erupted in gunplay when the youngest of the Harcourt brothers, Steve, stopped into Dunn's saloon and walked up to the bar where Dunn was serving customers. Steve was drunk. In a show of bravado, he ordered a drink and then told Danny to set up drinks for everyone in the house. Dunn refused. Steve took that as an opportunity to publicly berate Danny. The insults intensified and suddenly a whiskey bottle was involved in the fracas as a weapon. Steve stepped away from the bar in a rage. Suddenly a handgun was in his fist and he leveled it at Dunn. He pulled the trigger twice. The first bullet pierced Dunn's hand and the second impacted the wall behind him.

Dunn reached under the bar and retrieved the gun that he always kept handy before the sound of Steve's shot had died. He pointed his gun at

Steve and fired two rounds also. The first hit Steve in the neck and the second hit him in the abdomen. Witnesses remarked how Steve's blood spewed everywhere. He managed to escape before Dunn fired again and he staggered to his mother's house a few doors distant. Danny Dunn closed his bar and got on the next train to Manistique where he turned himself in to the sheriff. Meanwhile, the hapless Steve Harcourt lingered three days in his mother's house before he finally died. His death didn't seem to matter. The sheriff and prosecuting attorney believed Dunn's story and ruled the homicide as self-defense.

The Roscommon News provided their version of events in their June 26, 1891 edition. *"James Harcourt, who was visiting with his wife's parents, Mr. and Mrs. J Gardiner at Houghton Lake, was called to Seney last Saturday on receipt of a telegram announcing that his brother, Stephen, had been shot. From dispatches regarding the shooting it appears that Harcourt, who had been drinking, went over to Dunn's saloon and commenced a row, during which he drew a revolver and fired, the ball passing thought Dunn's left hand. Dunn returned the fire, the ball passing through Harcourt's body in the region of the abdomen. He staggered outdoors and commenced firing through the window and several more shots were fired one of which struck Steve in the face shattering his jaw and passing downward into his body. The wounded man was conveyed to his residence and a physician was summoned who made an examination but failed to locate the ball...."*

While Dunn was high-tailing it out of town, the five remaining Harcourt brothers had a meeting to decide which of them would avenge Steve's murder. After a lengthy discussion they decided that the only fair thing to do was to draw straws to see which of them would treat Dunn to the same fate that Steve suffered. The oldest brother, Jim, drew the shortest straw.

Roscommon had a strong pull on both the Harcourt family and Dan Dunn. On July 3rd, Steve Harcourt's remains were returned to Roscommon for burial. Dunn and the sheriff of Schoolcraft County also passed through Roscommon on the train – the sheriff was acting in the capacity of Dunn's bodyguard.

The Harcourt's seemed to have about the same level of bravado or stupidity as Dunn since they openly talked of the plan for Jim Harcourt to seek revenge on Dunn. The word got to Dunn shortly after his return from Manistique. He decided to ask the law for help and he contacted his favorite judge who agreed that the Harcourt's should be arrested to prevent further bloodshed. The sheriff was dispatched to Seney to arrest Jim Harcourt. When the sheriff met up with them, Jim and two of his brothers agreed to accompany the sheriff back to Manistique to talk with the judge about the case.

As luck would have it, Dunn had agreed to meet with his lawyer about the same time that the Harcourt's agreed to travel to Manistique. Dunn's lawyer suggested that he and Dunn meet in Trout Lake at a bar he knew. The train to Manistique stopped at Trout Lake, where the Manistique passengers had to wait for the next train. When the sheriff and the Harcourt brothers got off the train, someone suggested they have a drink while waiting for the train. As the group walked in the bar, Jim instantly recognized Dunn even though his back was turned toward him. Before anyone knew what was about to happen, Jim crossed the bar, pulled a 32 caliber pistol from his pocket and pointed it at Dunn's back, less than 2 feet distant. Bang! Bang! Bang! The sheriff stood silent with his mouth agape as Dunn fell forward and then slumped to the floor, stone dead.

Jim handed his gun to the sheriff and smiled at his brothers who each clapped him on the back. The party left the bar and went to the hotel where they had a pleasant supper with the brothers enjoying their good fortune in the killing of Dunn. After dinner, Jim was taken into custody by the sheriff and installed in the local jail. The Grayling Avalanche reported the murder.

Grayling Avalanche, July 30, 1891

"James Harcourt, brother of the man killed by Dan Dunn, shot and killed Dan in a saloon at Trout Lake, Monday. Dunn had been acquitted, at his examination last Saturday, hence his shooting by

*James Harcourt.   No one mourns his end, and it is a wonder he was
not killed long since."*

The Roscommon News was a little more circumspect in their reporting.

*"....Dunn had been acquitted ... on the charge of killing Harcourt and
had the three Harcourt boys, Dick, Tom and James, arrested on the
ground of threatening his life, and the sheriff and his prisoners were
on their way to Manistee for trial. The party were obliged to change
cars at Trout Lake and while waiting for their train stepped into Jack
Neyin's saloon. They stepped up to the bar and had a drink and Dunn
came into the room. He called for a drink and turned his back on the
Harcourt crowd when James drew his revolver and opened fire on
Dunn, three shots taking effect. One shot passed through the heart,
Dunn dying almost immediately. The sheriff released two of the
brothers and re-arrested James on the charge of murder and
proceeded to the Soo with his prisoner. It is no more than Dunn was
looking for, and he was foolish to take the chance he did, but at the
same time Harcourt is guilty of murder as he gave his victim no show,
shooting him in the back without warning."*

Danny's widow took charge of his corpse and arranged for his interment in
Detroit, the place where he had grown up. In short order Harcourt was
tried for murder, although the public sentiment seemed to be that he had
done the community a service. The jury found him guilty to a reduced
charge of manslaughter and the judge sentenced him to 10 years in state
prison.

Jim Harcourt's wife was a true believer in her husband. As soon as Jim was
behind bars she began her campaign to have his sentence reduced and
have Jim set free. She started writing letters and soon had help in getting
others to also write in support of Jim. She argued that Jim had actually
done a public service in the killing of Dunn and his due should have been
congratulations instead of incarceration. One of her many letters reached
the Governor who seemed favorably impressed with her arguments. The

Governor wrote a few letters of his own and soon the Advisory Board deliberated and filed this report.

Source: *Michigan Report of Prooceeding of the Advisory Board in the Matter of Pardons for the Year Ending December 31, 1898.* LANSING. 1899

JAMES HARCOURT. No. 313 (File No. 89).

The advisory board in the matter of pardons have had under consideration the application of James Harcourt, convicted of the crime of manslaughter, in the circuit court for the county of Chippewa, and now confined in prison at Marquette, for the term of two [SIC: ten] years from September 26, 1891—his prison number being 313— and we hereby submit our report and recommendation as follows: The facts in the case are that on or about June 24. 1891, Daniel Dunn shot and killed Stephen Harcourt. a brother of the applicant, in Dunn's saloon at Seney, Schoolcraft county. Shortly thereafter Dunn was arrested on the charge of murder and taken before a justice of the peace at Manistique, and there discharged after only a partial examination. As soon as Dunn was discharged, and before he left the justice's office, he paid Riggs, the prosecuting attorney of Schoolcraft county, quite a sum of money. It afterwards developed that the prosecuting attorney was more or less implicated in his discharge. Some time thereafter Riggs resigned his position and left the country. Dunn, immediately on being discharged, caused John Harcourt and Richard Harcourt, brothers of applicant, together with applicant, to be arrested, claiming that they had made threats against him. They were arrested at Seney on Sunday, July 26th. 1891. The sheriff started with them for Manistique, by way of Trout Lake Junction, where it was necessary to change cars, and while there waiting for the train for Manistique, the sheriff took the three Harcourt brothers to a saloon situated near the depot. Upon arriving at the saloon they all stepped up to the bar, and while there, Dunn, who had been occupying a room over the saloon, came down in his shirt sleeves with a revolver in his front right hand pants pocket, and passed up to the bar. He was told before reaching the foot of the stairs that the Harcourt brothers were in the bar-room and was asked not to come into the bar-room while they were there. It appears from the testimony that Dunn had threatened to shoot applicant on sight, and that such information had been conveyed to applicant, who was fully acquainted with Dunn's life and character, and believed that he would carry out his threats if he got the least opportunity. It satisfactorily appears from the evidence that applicant was standing at the farther end of the bar from the stairs, that he did not see Dunn when he came through the room, and not until applicant turned from the bar to go out of the door. At the same time Dunn turned his head, saw applicant and immediately reached for his revolver, and was in the very act of turning around and trying to get his revolver from his pocket, when applicant drew his revolver and, as he maintained, immediately shot to save his own life. Just before the shooting, the sheriff and John and Richard Harcourt had stepped out of the bar room, leaving applicant to make change at the bar. Dunn's revolver was partially out of his pocket when he fell, and another revolver was found in his right hand hip pocket.

A full stenographic report of all the evidence and proceedings had on the trial is on file in this case, and we have carefully examined the same. We find from it that Dunn was a desperate villain, and had been charged with several murders prior to the killing of applicant's brother. It also appears that he had been guilty of a number of unprovoked brutal assaults, and that he was proprietor of, and had kept for a number of years, a low dive, which was the resort of the most degraded women and toughs. He was a large powerful man, and had the reputation of always going armed, and of having no regard whatever for human life. He was frequently called "Dunn the cutter" from his practice of always being armed with a dangerous knife which he had used in his quarrels with other men. From the evidence in the case we conclude that Dunn was one of the most desperate and brutal villains that had ever disgraced the state. He had served time both at the State Prison and Detroit House of Correction.

It further appears that applicant is a man of medium size, and before the killing of Dunn always bore a good reputation and was a law-abiding and industrious citizen. Applicant's pardon has been recommended by a great number of reputable citizens of the locality in which he lived, and by prominent citizens all over the State, as will be seen by the numerous letters and petitions on file with the board, and to which we refer. It is further made to appear that the conviction could not have been obtained had the jury thought that so severe a sentence would be given and it is further claimed with reason that Harcourt would have been acquitted altogether but for the fact that a man charged with murder in Chippewa county had a few months prior to applicant's trial been found not guilty, but had subsequently confessed, creating in the community a strong sentiment against any person charged with the crime.

After a most thorough examination of all the testimony given on the trial, and the evidence before the board, we are convinced that the shooting of Dunn by applicant was justifiable. We therefore respectfully recommend, in consideration of the premises, that a pardon be granted.

Even the Michigan legislature responded to the entreaties and provided their view as follows;

Journal of the Senate, State of Michigan, 1897, Vol. I, Page 50

JAMES HARCOURT.

State House of Correction and Branch of the State Prison in the Upper Peninsula at Marquette. Convicted in the circuit court for the county of Chippewa, of manslaughter, and sentenced for ten years from September 19, 1891. Sentence commuted May 6, 1895, so as to expire May 8, 1895. While the evidence at the trial failed to convince the jury that the shooting was strictly in self defense, it does show that Harcourt had reason to believe that Dunn would shoot him at the first opportunity. After a thorough investigation of this case the conclusion has been reached that in view of all the circumstances Harcourt has been sufficiently punished for the offense. This position is sustained by the recommendation of the jury before whom he was tried, by two separate and distinct pardon boards and by a very large number of prominent citizens of the State, acquainted with the two men and with the circumstances of the shooting. Interested friends have raised a small amount of money to aid him to start anew in life, far from the scenes of his past life, where he will follow an entirely different occupation from that in which he was formerly engaged.

The words from the Senate were prophetic. The freed Harcourt went on to live an exemplary life, staying out of trouble and living as a responsible citizen.

Shortly after Dunn was killed, his saloon was torched and burned to the ground. Within a few months, the main lumber company in town announced that it was moving it's saw mill and offices from Seney to Grand Marais in the chase for the remaining logs. The town began a slow descent after that. As the logs and lumber played out, the camps disappeared and only the memory of Danny Dunn, the pimp, murderer, and saloon keeper from Roscommon, lived on in the shadow of the stumps that graced the area. By then, Roscommon's boom times had also passed into history and no one mourned Danny, John Mahoney or Sadie and few understood the short lives they led amid the booze and high times and the money that did them no good in the end.

Roscommon buckled under the loss of most of its forests and only the determination and stamina of a few men and women and a little luck kept the town alive and, if not quite thriving, at least kept the town going. It continued as county seat and a center of living for the remaining lumbermen and farmers who struggled to earn a livelihood and make a life among the many stumps scattered all about the lakes and rivers.

Chapter 12

Roscommon Life in 1880's

Roscommon life in the 1880's was different than anything most of us can imagine. Everything was harder: traveling, staying clean, staying healthy, keeping warm, and so forth. The demands of everyday life in the 1880's were so much more difficult and so different than 21st century life that a simple recounting of life experiences can hardly do justice to this time period in Roscommon. A summary of differences between then and now can begin to help. A start on a long list would begin by noting that the average life span was 42 years. More babies died, more children became ill and died, and adults passed away much earlier because of injury and illnesses that were either untreated or untreatable in that time.

A short of list of some things not yet available in 1880 may help the reader: efficient home heating and cooling systems, refrigeration and modern food preservation, safe and effective medical care, comfortable transportation, indoor plumbing, and water at the twist of a knob. The business of living in 1880 required energy, stamina, and a tolerance for discomfort that would surprise most of us.

The period of the 1880's was known as the Victorian Age for Queen Victoria of England who reigned during this period. In spite of their disdain for 'the old country' members of America's upper class mimicked high society in England in their clothing style, manners, and moral behavior. As always, the upper reaches of society set the standard and those below tried to follow in their footsteps. The Victorian Age reached Roscommon just as surely as it did New York City, a little later and with less vigor perhaps, but with the same impact on the culture of the small lumbering community.

Clothing of the period was formal and stiff and careful attention was paid to every detail of each garment, especially women's clothing which covered the entire body (even the glimpse of an ankle was scandalous). Stiff, confining corsets were required wear for women during formal affairs as females tried to show off waists that were as small as possible to accent hips and bosoms by comparison. The clothing completely covered their bodies with large flowing skirts that were worn over layers of petticoats for formal occasions.

Queen Victoria in an Elaborate Gown

Ladies' clothes for everyday wear mimicked the styles set for formal wear: everyday dresses were floor length affairs, elaborate hats were common and high top shoes completed the outfit even though they were rarely seen beneath the long dresses. Females had to manage wearing these clothes for all activities, even demanding household chores and there were lots of those, especially for women on the farm. Most days started early and ended late and involved caring for a family and animals that were essential.

The traditional 'woman's work' was extensive and involved food preparation, care and cleaning of the home, washing people and clothes, providing medical care when needed, caring for some of the animals, preserving food, and gardening. These tasks required the hard, heavy work of toting water, carrying firewood, digging in the soil and other tasks demanding a strong body – it was not for sissies although the fashions of the day demanded that they look as if they led a life of leisure.

1880's Woman on the Farm with Chickens – Life Magazine Photo

Only the wealthiest people in 1880 had the time and inclination for leisure time events involving sport. And of these, men were by far those who were most often involved in a sporting or leisure activity such as running, hunting, horse racing, base ball, and other events demanding strength, speed and agility.

Sport involving females was rare, and if engaged in, it was more likely to be considered a genteel sport involving social interaction with others. Lawn games like croquet and tennis and the lake and seashore activity of swimming were considered suitable female diversions if the female were properly attired.

Tennis Players in 1880 – Life Magazine Photo

Men's clothing in 1880 was equally formal, but similar to earlier styles with three piece suits of dark colors being commonly worn. Hats, often Homburgs, were virtually always worn no matter what the weather. Business men often showed how important they were and their careful managing of time by displaying large pocket watch chains dangling from a vest pocket.

The Victorian emphasis on style was demonstrated by household furnishings as well as dress. Here, ornate, heavy drapes and ornamentation of all types were everywhere evident. Furniture was covered with dark fabrics and windows were ornamented with lacy curtains. Even lamps bore fancy, decorative lampshades often with tassels hanging low for all to admire.

The trend for heavy ornamentation continued with the exterior of homes being layered with added touches that were purely ornamental. Porches with elaborate railings and showy facades featuring whimsical curlicues of one type or another became common. Roof lines were transformed with a combination of turrets, gables, false fronts and false chimneys. Houses were even painted with bright and contrasting colors to add accent and style to certain features of the house that the householder wanted to show off. For those wealthy enough, homes became showplaces as well as domiciles.

Roscommon Post Office Around 1880 with the Properly Attired Employee Ms. Snively

One of the things that came directly from Queen Victoria was an insistence on proper behavior especially as it pertained to things sexual. Proper Victorian manners required a universal charade that banned the existence of sex, childbirth, sweat, defecation and any of a number of other unpleasant personal matters. One simply did not speak publicly about sex, childbirth, and other such matters and any reference to them at all had to be carefully camouflaged with a number of coded euphemistic expressions. Even the medical profession had a difficult time in polite society.

These Victorian cultural standards came into direct conflict with the frontier area of northern Michigan in the 1880's. Those arriving in Roscommon during this period were of hardy American stock or recently arrived immigrants who had experienced the hard, gritty side of life and had little time or money for the nuances of polite society. At the same time, they longed for the wealth and status that the upper classes represented.

The United States began as a largely rural nation, with most people living on farms or in small towns and villages. While the rural population continued to grow in the late 1800s, the urban population was growing more rapidly. Still, a majority of Americans lived in rural areas in the 1880's and most of those who came to Roscommon shared that rural, farm background. Farming was by far and away the single largest occupation in America – almost 50% of the population lived and worked on a farm.

New machines for use in farming were invented in this period, but horses, oxen, and people still provided most of the power that operated the machinery. While some farmers produced cash crops (crops grown for sale), many grew crops and animals for their own use. These folks were remarkably self-sufficient, making or trading for nearly everything required by their families. Vegetable gardens were common even for those who lived in the settlements; nearly everyone found enough space around their house to work up what soil they had for planting a few vegetables.

Most farms were worked by farm families where the children were an important labor source. All shared in the work including the very youngest who were given jobs they could do such as feeding chickens, helping in the kitchen, and so forth. The work needed to operate a household was huge by the standards of the 21st century: staying warm, preparing food, and keeping clean were difficult tasks in the days when that demanded carrying firewood for the stove, pumping and carrying water for the kitchen, and heating water for washing one's self and one's clothes. Many of life's daily tasks involved a measure of discomfort as well. Early morning trips to the privy during the winter months when the path was snow covered and the seat was cold and hard was just one of many minor discomforts.

The school year for children often followed the cycle of work on a farm. Boys were especially needed during the harvest season to help in the fall harvest and so school was typically delayed until the harvest was completed.

Getting Ready to Fork Hay in the Haymow

Children were exposed to all facets of life on the farm from husbandry to butchering. The earthy business of installing and occasionally moving the privy was known to all including the youngest and most 'outhouses' had multiple seats so that it could be used by more than one person at a time. Victorian sensibilities may have been offended but in farm families it was sometimes necessary for even the youngest children to attend and assist in a difficult birth of livestock.

The remote areas of some farms and the difficulty in transportation demanded that farm families be self-sufficient in the matter of caring for themselves. This included the need to care for those who fell ill and thus a variety of home remedies were used, some of which made the patient sicker. Sometimes patients claimed improvement to avoid further treatment. Teas made from catnip and sassafras were believed helpful for some ailments while turpentine and sugar was given for worms. One 1880's woman recalled her mother's treatments with a degree of longing, "Turpentine and lard rubbed on the chest was wonderful for colds, and if we had no turpentine we could use coal oil or kerosene…." "We also had several kinds of poultices, flax seed poultice, bread and milk poultice, and beefsteak poultice which my mother put on me whenever I came home with a black eye. But the very best poultice for sores was the angle worm poultice. It would draw all the smart out of even a bad felon. The worms were taken alive, placed upon the sore, and wrapped around with a bandage. For earache sometimes mother used laudanum dropped into the ear with a dropper. There were pain killer pills to be got at the store, but the usual remedy for headaches was hot or cold packs applied to the head. For burns, she made a paste of bicarbonate of soda and water and spread it over the burned area. Too, as soon as one was burned it was always best for him to hold the burn as close to the heat as possible and quickly as possible. This would hurt something dreadful but it would draw all the fire out almost at once."

Professional medical help in the 1880's was sometimes not much better that the home remedies noted above. The same woman who recalled her mother's remedies with turpentine sadly recalled the death of her brother. "Sometimes people were dosed with straight turpentine, as in the case of my brother who died of diphtheria. It was the doctor who doped him, and he gave him too much."

Medical science in 1880 was still fragmentary at best. Doctors of the time had widely varying amounts of training and many had learned their skills at the hands of older doctors who had even less training and little education. Effective medicines were few and far between and many doctors used medications that were based on 'natural' remedies, that is, they were little better than the home remedies noted above. Doctors of the time also used opiates to provide relief from pain and to help control spasms and coughing. Popular drugs that had opiate effects were paregoric, laudanum, opium and morphine. No legal controls were exercised for the use of these drugs and they were available for purchase by anyone who wanted them.

For a time, Roscommon had an Indian who was known to abuse alcohol. He operated a drug store and advertised that he was a physician and surgeon. It must have been a brave person who ventured into his small shop for surgery.

Common injuries could become major health problems. The Roscommon newspaper commented on one such example with such a casual attitude to suggest that such occurrences were common.

"Courtney Wallace, while under the influence of liquor, fell on the sidewalk and broke his leg. It was not believed serious initially, but it may prove fatal." -***The Roscommon News***, **Feb 4, 1887**

Roscommon citizens, like others of the era, sought relief from the pain and aggravations of daily life by self-medication when possible. As a result, large profits could be made in the sales of generally worthless tonics, pills, creams, balms, plasters, and treatments of one sort or another that were touted for pain relief or cures. *The Roscommon News* was full of advertisements for these so-called remedies; 25 of 46 ads in one issue were for "Tutt's Liver Pills," "Burlock's Blood Bitters," "St. Jacobs Oil for Pain" and other equally marvelous curatives.

The combined result of the lack of medical knowledge and the lifestyle of the time was short lifespans. Although some people lived a full, healthy life until their 70's or 80's, most succumbed much earlier to injury or accident or an illness that couldn't be controlled. The United States average lifespan in 1880 was 42 years for men and 44 for women.

Roscommon News Ad for a Blood Tonic, Dec. 4, 1885

Much of Roscommon food for most meals was of the meat and potatoes genre. Fish and game were common fare and were taken locally from the forests and streams in the area. A lady who grew up in that era comments, *"Our food was pretty plain most of the time and we didn't have any salads like they do now. The menu for a fine dinner would be: Chicken stew with dumplings, mashed potatoes, peach preserves, biscuits, and hominy. We raised carrots for the stock but we never thought of eating them. . . . We didn't have any jars to put up preserves in, like they do now, but we used earthen crooks instead. The fruit to be preserved was boiled with brown sugar -- we never saw white sugar and when we did we used it as candy -- and then put in the jars which were covered with cloth that was then coated with beeswax. Another good cover was a hog bladder -- they were the best. Sometimes we had molasses pulls and once in a great while we would have some real striped, candy. That was a treat!"*

The Michigan Central Railroad provided some of foodstuffs that couldn't be grown locally such as oranges and other citrus fruit. One delicacy that seemed to be widely enjoyed based on restaurant and grocery advertisements was oysters. Even though Roscommon folks were far from the source of such food, they seemed to take pleasure in having these delights from the seas most seasons of the year.

The menu from a fancy dinner that was hosted at the Pioneer House in 1887 was as follows:

Appetizer – Oysters, stewed or raw

Cold meats – turkey and chicken

Entrée – boiled ham with hot rolls and butter

Relishes – chicken salad, cabbage salad, jellied chicken, tomato, mixed pickles

Pastry – fruit cake, orange cake, lemon cake, coconut cake, chocolate cake, Sugar Tops

Dessert – orange jelly, wine jelly, Lemon Sponge, apples and oranges

Drinks – tea, coffee, sweet milk

As usual, the *Roscommon News* commented on the affair, *"The Dinner and Dance held at the Pioneer House held in celebration of Washington's Birthday was the largest event of this type ever held in Roscommon. The able managers of the Pioneer House, Mr. and Mrs. A. H. Blanchard, hosted a dinner for 175 people who danced until the early hours."*

The people who attended the party were generally younger and they worked hard and played hard. The newspaper went on to note that the affair was attended by folks from St. Helen as well as Roscommon. Those from St. Helen had to leave early to catch the 2:00 AM train for home.

Farmers from the outlying areas of the county had to rely on their own means for transportation, typically their horse and buggy. The roads were uniformly bad so getting home in bad weather could be a problem. Accordingly, many of the farm families came to town only when necessary for essential supplies. Fortunately, supplies occasionally came to them via the post office or by an itinerant peddler who traveled down farm roads with a wagon loaded with goods. The other option for farm families to purchase goods came from that marketing genius, Aaron Montgomery Ward, who developed a catalog that came to be universally known as the 'Wish Book.'

Aaron Montgomery Ward was an experienced salesman and store manager when he and his brother-in-law established the first mail-order firm to carry a wide variety of goods in 1872. Ward's catalog gave farmers an option to the general stores in town and allowed goods to be delivered directly to the nearest post office. Montgomery Ward and Company quickly became the leading mail-order house in the United States until 1900, when it was surpassed by Sears, Roebuck and Company. The company later expanded and opened branch stores in the 1920s, ultimately discontinuing its catalog operation.

Ward began to think of starting his own mail-order business when he was a traveling salesman. He became well acquainted with the rural way of life in the Midwest and the needs of farmers and other residents. Their biggest complaint, he discovered, was the high prices they paid for goods at the local general stores. In addition, the selection of merchandise offered by the stores was meager at best. He decided to solve that problem and Ward's Wish Book was born to the delight of many families first in the Midwest, and later across the country.

Folks in Roscommon in the 1880's had a range of entertainment opportunities that were typical of small towns throughout America; community celebrations for the 4th of July, Washington's Birthday and other patriotic affairs was a large part of local life. One long lasting and important affair was the annual meeting of veterans from the Civil War. Those who participated had a special bond for one another.

The Roscommon Opera House provided entertainment with an occasional professional traveling show. Other performances by local talent were also featured at the Opera House. A regular performing group was The Roscommon Band, a small brass band of local talent that was funded by the community. The band needed regular infusions of cash to pay for their teacher and they arranged solicitations from the community. An unusual fund drive was held in 1886: *"The Roscommon Band Social was held to provide financial support for the band and their eminent teacher, Professor Corrazi. The fund raising social included a dinner and a contest to determine the handsomest female in attendance. The results of the voting were:*

Olive Nash – 301 votes

Nettie Hamilton – 1

Nellie Murphy – 7

Maggie Martin – 5

Carrie Fox – 148

The net receipts for the evening were $65. This makes a grand success for the band and ensures their continued training under Professor Corrazi."

Nellie, Nettie and Maggie must have been disappointed. It is insightful of the times that the newspaper felt the need to report the results of the lopsided vote on the matter of personal beauty regardless of the impact on the young ladies.

Roscommon Band in Front of The Pioneer House

(Photo from Roscommon Centennial Publication)

Recreation of different sort was afforded by the lakes and the streams and forests in the area that provided opportunities for hunting and fishing, an endeavor that was as common a preoccupation then as now, as many folks spent their leisure time in pursuit of either finned and/or furred creatures.

Roscommon people also created their own diversions and the events were often reported by the News.

"An excursion was held on the recently completed railroad from Harrison to Houghton Lake at Prudenville. After the excursion, 200 people boarded the steamer, Little Jake for a pleasant boat ride on the lake. The partygoers then finished the evening with a dinner at either the Pruden House or Harcourt's Hotel." **The Roscommon News, July 23, 1886**

Card playing, visiting, and partying was common and was reported by the Roscommon News. Another diversion was roller skating at "The Rink." The village had a roller skating rink that vied for skaters by arranging any number of events; races, endurance skating, skating exhibitions, and so forth. Even though The Rink seemed barely able to remain profitable as the business closed and then changed hands during the period, it appeared to attract reputable citizens who were looking for wholesome entertainment.

The village also contained a bowling alley. This form of entertainment was likely oriented for the lumberjacks as it featured a companion bar owned by a man named Jack Nevins. For one period, Nevins was in partnership with a notorious roughneck named Danny Dunn as noted in Chapter 11.

An 1880's Card Party – Life Magazine Photo

'Base ball' was another of the diversions enjoyed by Roscommon people during the period as the town hosted their own team of amateur players. The game was still in its infancy and the fact that it existed at all was something of a gift of the Civil War. Before the war a number of games like base ball were played at various places but each locality seemed to have its own rules, resulting in continuing disputes. During the war, soldiers from all around the country played together. Gradually, a set of rules evolved that standardized the game and allowed Roscommon players to compete with teams from Grayling and elsewhere.

The 1880 rules were different than the rules used today. A walk occurred after seven balls (not four) and the umpire asked the batter where he would like the ball before the pitcher let fly. "Gentlemanly" behavior was insisted upon from the single umpire who ruled the game while standing behind the pitcher, sometimes smoking a cigar as was also allowed by the rules.

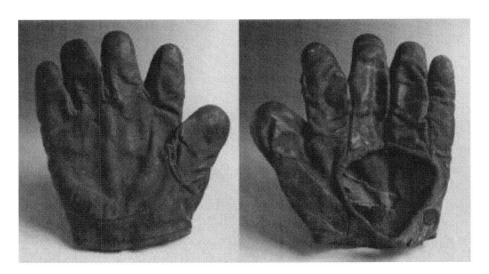

Baseball Glove from the late 19th Century

Local competing teams were not always totally amateur. Wealthy lumbermen Tom Stephens and Rasmus Hansen were fans of the game and each supported a local team. At season's end, each arranged to "import" skilled professional players for a series of local games constituting a play-off. Stephens won the game of 'one-ups-manship' when he hired Detroit's Ty Cobb to come north for a series of games.

1880s-Baseball-game-

Outdoor activities were popular both winter and summer. Ice skating and riding toboggans were both in vogue. St. Helen was said to have the largest toboggan slide anywhere in the north and the newspaper reported a crowd of 1,200 people attended the opening run. Prudenville also had a toboggan that attracted its share of riders.

Prices and wages were both low during the period. Wages at the saw mills and the lumber camps were relatively stable and the jacks earned a salary of $1 per day at every camp in northern Michigan. Teamsters earned more because they worked longer hours and many owned their own team of horses. Blacksmiths and other skilled worked also earned more than the jacks and the top camp worker, the foreman could earn as much as $5 per day.

Prices were correspondingly low: a restaurant meal or a church benefit dinner could be had for 25 cents. An excursion on the train from Roscommon Station to Bay City was $1.25 for a round trip ticket.

The low prices at the market benefitted consumers. A depression had occurred after 1865 resulting in low prices for consumer goods while most wages had remained pretty much the same thus providing a bargain for buyers.

	1865 Prices	**1885 Prices** (in dollars)
6.5 lb Pork	1.25	.44
6 lb Butter	2.1	1.2
11 lb codfish	1.78	1.13
½ lb tea	.75	.30
1 bbl flour	12.00	5.00
1 spool thread	.10	.05
1 peck potatoes	.13	.08
10 Lbs sugar	1.70	.80

The life of a worker in Roscommon revolved principally around the lumbering business. Farmers sold their grain, vegetables and livestock to support the camps, while the merchants provided goods and entertainment for the farmer as well as the camp workers. A limited opportunity existed to earn a living outside the lumber business.

During the warmer months, the area hosted tourists for hunting and fishing and a few local people sold and shipped huckleberries and deer. Some years the huckleberry crop was enormous as the plants grew in the cut-over forests and the locals spent weeks harvesting the tiny berries for distant markets.

Everyday life in Roscommon must have seemed pleasant in the 1880's as the county and its small towns enjoyed the growth and prosperity brought by the lumbering industry. Prices were low, wages were stable and there was work for everyone. The changes provoked by the Victorian Age were probably welcomed since they were coincident with the robust economy. In any case, the changes in polite society were small compared to the gigantic changes happening to the landscape all the around the county as the lumbermen denuded the forests in every direction.

Chapter 13

Newspaper Reports

Roscommon had the good fortune to be served by a succession of newspapers during its formative years. The first newspaper, The Roscommon Co. Pioneer, sprouted in Houghton Lake not much after the first wave of settlers had become established in the remote north woods. It was published by a man named Frank Matthews beginning in 1876. When the village of Roscommon became the county seat in 1879, Matthews moved his paper to that village.

The village of Roscommon was served by its own paper, The Roscommon News. From 1880 to 1885, the village had two newspapers, one Republican and the other Democratic. As lumbering and business began to subside after 1885, The Roscommon County Pioneer fell on hard times and folded, leaving only The Roscommon News. The News was initially owned by the Bay City Tribune until the Ward Bros., James and Robert, completed their purchase of the paper in 1885. The Roscommon Herald began publishing their paper on Dec. 19, 1907 by The Herald Publishing Co.

Unfortunately, none of the papers published before 1885 have survived. Digital copies of The Roscommon News are available at the Roscommon District Library for dates after June, 1885 although several issues from the turn of the century were destroyed by fire.

In 1885 The Roscommon News was a weekly, four page newspaper dedicated to providing news and advertising for the entire county. "The Official Paper of the County" they announced proudly in their masthead, although it was never clear just who had made it so. The paper did enjoy the county's business as they signed a contract each year to print the required legal notices that the county was obliged to publicize.

December 4, 1885 Issue of *The Roscommon News*

During the boom period of 1880's the paper enjoyed local, regional, and national advertising that amounted to 40 – 50 percent of the paper's white space. The balance was given to news; national, state and local. The national and state news came from wire services but the local news was obtained in the time-honored way involving the publisher's shoe leather or by personal visits to the newspaper office of those who wanted to see their name in the paper.

The owner and publisher of the News was R. W. Ward and Co. They began the paper in affiliation with the Bay City newspaper, The Tribune. In November of 1885 the Ward's purchased their paper from its Bay City owners and modestly announced, "The Ward Brothers have completed their purchase of the Roscommon News having paid off the Bay City Tribune." (Nov. 27, 1885) In May of 1888 the newspaper increased its size from four pages to eight in order to "enlarge our patronage." Their timing was poor, as the lumbering in Roscommon slowed during the latter part of the decade, advertising space in the paper fell also. During that same month, the newspaper noted that "we enter into 14 years of existence in Roscommon County."

A Line Drawing in a 1888 Edition

The early papers were were devoid of artwork except for advertising copy that came to the News from state and national sources. All local copy consisted of text only, although the ads showed an artistic side with the use of a variety of font styles and white space to attract interest. The first artwork depicting pictures in conjunction with news stories began in the latter part of the 1880's when line drawings began to be used to illustrate stories. Again, this artwork came from state or national sources.

In addition to advertising revenue and subscription fees, The News also derived income by publishing those legal notices required by law and the required official county reports. These matters were printed either on the first or last page. Local news took top billing on the front page but without the use of headlines. Curiously, the top local news appeared under the front page heading 'Editorial' and the balance of local news appeared on the last page.

If nothing else, the Ward's and their staff were hard-working publishers, perhaps a reflection of the work habits of their customers. They published a full paper on Christmas Day, 1885 without missing a beat. During the week of the 1885 Thanksgiving Day they noted that the stores would be open on Thanksgiving but closed from 1:30 to 4:00 PM to mark the occasion. Such were the work habits of the Roscommon citizenry.

The local news included a wide variety of items including disguised advertising, rumor, gossip, hearsay, and unattributed reports from the editors about local people and local happenings. Many of the stories are humorous, some are sad, and all shed light on the demanding, vigorous life in the county in 1880's. The reports were always painfully brief and without background or context, the editor assuming that readers already understood what he knew. The newspaper office was not above selling small things for a profit also. Most editions of the paper offered a "reins holder to keep your reins from the dirt" that could be purchased in the newspaper office.

Above everything else, during the 1880's the newspaper kept a running account of any news about lumbering; the Ward Brothers understood that lumbering was the lifeblood of the county. Even with the lumbering reports however, the pieces written were brief and lacked detail for a reader more than 100 years later, hence some explanatory information is needed for an understanding of the records.

1. **"Put In"** intended to mean the cut logs were ready to be "put in" the lake or river for transport to the mill for sawing. The newspaper sometimes used the term "put in" to mean the logs were banked for shipment even if the shipment was by rail.
2. **"Two million or 2 M (or any number) "** used to denote the number of board feet of lumber that could be made from the cut logs. See chapter 6, page 10 for more detail)
3. **"Dray haul"** transporting logs by wagon.
4. **"Team**" a team of horses or oxen used for pulling sleds or wagons. Oxen were originally used for hauling but horses were able to pull heavier loads and were more adept at following commands, thus most camps gravitated to their use.
5. **"Joe Smith is putting in logs for XYZ Company**" Joe Smith is the jobber being paid by a lumbering company, usually a saw mill, to cut and deliver logs to the mill.
6. **"Driving"** (the logs) creating a raft of logs and pulling them to the river or escorting them down the river.
7. **"River Hogs" or "Drivers" also sometimes called the "Push" or "pushers"** the men employed in driving logs

Driving the logs on Higgins Lake

(Photo from Roscommon Centennial Publication)

This barge was used to pull rafts of logs across Higgins Lake to the Cut River to be floated to Houghton Lake where a steamer would pull logs to the Muskegon River. The horse standing on the raft walked in a circle and reeled in a line that was attached to an anchor thus pulling the raft forward. The small boat was used to carry the anchor forward before the horse went to work.

The year of 1885 saw Roscommon lumbermen at the peak of their work in cutting logs for lumber. After this peak, lumber volumes began to decline as prime forest areas for cutting were consumed. The total volume cut in Roscommon in 1885 was an astounding amount. Since the data given in the newspaper doesn't specify the precise area where cutting occurred, some small portion of the volumes listed below may have been taken from adjacent counties. Nevertheless, the reports listed below total a mind-boggling record of more than 145 million board feet of logs cut from Roscommon County in one season – enough lumber to build nearly 100 buildings each the size of the Grand Hotel! The lumber made from these logs was shipped by the mills to markets in the both the east and west, principally Chicago and Albany, New York.

A Northern Michigan Logging Camp

Here are the most significant of the 1885/86 winter season lumbering reports from the *Roscommon News* in the language used by the Ward Brothers.

Sept. 1885: "An attempt is being made to operate a ten hour law in the lumber woods." The article explained how previous work by lumberjacks was based on the daylight hours. The men worked from sunup to sundown at a wage of one dollar a day. The hours worked therefore varied with the time of year, there being considerably more daylight in the summer months than during the winter. Since logging was done mostly during winter, their hours varied from late fall work till early spring, but averaged around 10 hours per day – the same as the working hours in the saw mill. After some while, the ten hour day became a standard work day. The news story went on to point out that teamsters in the logging camps were generally higher paid than the jacks since they worked longer hours, preparing the roads before dawn and caring for the horses at the end of the work day.

"Mr. Geel anticipates no trouble in securing all the men he needs that will make agreements releasing him from liability for extra compensation in the spring. He believes the contract system (for ten hour days at $1 per day) should be adhered to in order to prevent the men being induced to commence (legal) proceedings when they come out (of the woods in spring). None of the men whom we have seen anticipate any trouble in getting men when they are ready for operation."

"B. Geel who is lumbering on the main stream of the Au Sable has a 10,000,000 job (or 10 M) for the Moore Lumber Co, was in the village and informs us that he has one camp in operation and expects to start another soon."

"Mr. B. Geel was in the village Tuesday from his camp down on the main branch of the Au Sable where he is engaged in putting in a large tract of pine in which he has an interest for Moore. He details the passage down the S. Branch from here …" The story goes on to explain that Geel had loaded a boat that was 45 feet long and 14 feet wide with 15 tons of gear for his lumber camp. Geel had made arrangements for the dam at St. Helen to be opened to supply flood waters to enable his craft to negotiate the shallows of the South Branch. He explained that the boat was floated successfully till the craft reached the "Atwood Rapids" at which point it ran hard aground."

"Geel said that the teamsters removed about four tons of gear before the boat was able to be floated and he hired a team to carry the excess load. On balance he felt that this first attempt to carry supplies in this manner proved "entirely satisfactory" and he plans to send another load in about three weeks in the same manner. The story noted that one disadvantage of this means of conveyance of camp supplies was the opening of the dam and the resulting problem this created for farmers who wanted to make hay from the marsh grass that grew alongside the stream."

"Edward Nelson, supervisor of Roscommon Township has taken a job of putting in 2,000,000 feet of logs for S. C. Hall of Muskegon. The logs will be banked on the Muskegon, in the vicinity of Boiling Springs. Mr. Nelson will only run one camp, it being all dray haul."

Oct. 1885: Several worker strikes were noted across the state and particularly at sawmills in Saginaw and Bay City as result of the ten hour law.

"L.G.Mason of Muskegon, in giving his opinion on the ten hour law says, 'I now run my mills in accordance with the state law and I turn our just as much lumber a day as I did before. The machinery runs faster and the men work a little harder but when they quit at night they are not so tired as under the old system of 11 hours."

"L.W. Knapp of Roscommon Township informs us that he will begin lumbering in about ten days. He has about 500,000 feet to put in. He will bank them on Houghton Lake."

"Wm. Morrison is busily building camps on section T24 R3 west where he has taken a job of putting in 2.5 M for A. Betrand. The logs will be banked on Higgins Lake."

Nov. 1885: Here are the suppliers to the lumber camps:

- E. Kiely & Co. supplies camps for: J. Campbell, M Laughray, O.S. Davis, A Olsen, Wm Horison ,J.S. Mc Crae.
- Blodgett & Byrne supplies camps for C. Blanchard, P Dickson, B & B camps 1 & 3, J.M. & Co, camps 8 & 9
- John Tracey supplies Geo Fuller, B.O. Geel, Samuel Sias

<u>Logging Notes</u>

What the various firms will put in this winter

1. Blodgett & Byrne will put in 25 M (million board feet of logs) into the Muskegon River over their logging road which is called the Portage Lake and Muskegon railroad. They have 18 miles of road besides several branches. They have three camps and employ 200 men.
2. O. P. Dickinson is putting 250,000 into the "Cut" (now known as the Cut River) for Blodgett & Byrne.
3. Charles Lamonte is putting 250,000 into the "Cut" for Blodgett & Byrne and 500,000 for Capt. J. D. Woodbury.
4. Laughrey Bros., who are running camp some eight miles south of this village will put in 3.5 M for Johnathan Boyce of Muskegon. These logs go into the Cut. John Laughrey, of the above firm, will put in 500,000 into the Cut for himself.
5. Charles Blanchard & Co. have a contract of putting in 2 M into Higgins Lake for the Petrie Lumber Company of Muskegon.
6. L. W. Knapp is putting into Houghton Lake 500,000 feet of pine for himself.
7. N. H. Evans has two small jobs, one of 400,000 for A. Bertrand and one of 250,000 for Capt. J. D. Waterbury. These logs go into Higgins Lake.
8. Edw. Nelson will put in 2 M for S. C. Hall into the Muskegon.
9. John Murray will put in 10 M on the Cut.
10. J. Campbell will put in 3 M. These logs go into the Higgins Lake and Muskegon waters.
11. Alan Olsen is putting in 3 M, O.S. Lewis 1.5 M, D. A. Shumway 1 M for the Ducey Lumber Co. These logs all go into Muskegon waters.
12. J. B. McCrae is putting into the South Branch 1.5 M for the Moore Lumber Co.
13. L. J. Miller is putting in 500,000 for the Moore Lumber Co. He banks his logs on the South Branch of the Au Sable.
14. Wm. Tierney [Terney] has a contract of putting in 4 M for the same company. He also banks his logs on the South Branch.

15. W. W. Vaughn will put into the South Branch 700,000 for himself, he having lately made a purchase of a piece of pine some miles northeast of this village.
16. Jack Malone is also putting in 500,000 into the South Branch.
17. B. Geel is putting in for himself and H. C. Moore 10 M. These logs go into the main branch of the Au Sable.
10. Wm. Morrison of Mt. Pleasant, has a job of putting in 3 M into Higgins Lake for E. Bertrand of Muskegon. His camp is just one mile west of the village.
11. M. Wilson will put in 5 M into the Cut and Houghton Lake.
12. A.H. Knappen will also put 500,000 into Houghton Lake.
13. M. Bresnaham has taken a job of putting in 500,000 into Higgins Lake for S. W. Turner.
14. Duncan Cameron is putting 1 M into Backus Creek for the S. C. Hall lumber company.
15. Stimson, Fay & Co. of Muskegon are putting 1 M into Houghton Lake at Chappell's Landing.
16. C. B Field, for the Roscommon Lumber Co. will put into Houghton Lake over their logging road 25 M.
17. The A. W. Wright Lumber Co. will put in some 10M of their own timber and will probably put in as much for other parties.
18. Wells, Stone & Co., we are informed, will put in 25 M
19. H. Stephens & Co. of St Helen will put in 25 or 30 M.
20. Geo. Hartman, who is lumbering on the Au Sable, is putting in 1.5 M for the Panoyer Bros. of the Au Sable.

"An informed observer has advised of logging volumes expected for 1886 from the Muskegon mills. They expect to order 600 M logs with the largest of the mills ordering up to 35 M. Larger orders are expected from Ducey Lumber, Rynerson Hills & Co. Blodgett &Byrne, Porrent & Arms."

Another Large Pine Deal

"Mr. Jonathon Boyer of Grand Rapids who has been engaged in the lumber business in Muskegon for years was in our city today. He was asked if he knew of any large business deals. "The only one I know of is the one I concluded a few hours ago. I have purchased from O. P. Pillsbury& Co. a

tract of pine in Roscommon County which is estimated to cut above 50 M"
It is located in 24 north 2 west. It adjoins a piece of property that I have
owned for some years. The price, $210,000 for 2,280 acres or $92 an acre.
'That makes about 10,000 acres I have in that vicinity, nearly all of it in
Roscommon County that should net around 200 M feet of logs (equivalent
to 88,000 board feet per acre). I expect to build a railroad of eleven miles
to bring the logs to the Muskegon River.'"

Jan 29, 1886 "W. J. Terney says there will be in the neighborhood of 12 M
feet put in Higgins Lake this season for Muskegon. Rumor has it that C.
Blanchard will do the driving."

Feb 5, 1886 "150 M more logs will be put in the Muskegon River this year
over last year, about 600 M total. The capacity of the 3 mills in Muskegon is
640 M Camp wages are 20$ per month average."

Feb 26, 1886 "Henry Stephens died in California. He was nearly 60 years of
age. He had left his lumber business in the hands of his sons. He owned
timber in Wisconsin & Minnesota, cattle and sheep ranches in Wyoming,
mines in Colorado and real estate in various places. He left a widow, two
sons and a daughter, Mrs. Mc Ivor"

March 26, 1886 "Lots of men in town. The saloons are having a harvest
now."

"W. J. Tierney [Terney] finished up his job down the railroad some 7 mile
south of this place. He reported great results: no sickness and 4 M put in.
He is contemplating a dray haul and should he undertake it, he may move
his family to Roscommon."

April 2, 1886- James Watson has taken the contract for driving logs on
Higgins Lake and the Cut, the amount of logs being 20M. He started up
business and he will employ a force of 100 men, 20 on the lake and 80 on
the river. Jerry Woelowen will be the 'push' on the river and Mike Ryan on
the lake.

April 16, 1886 - Several citizens have subscribed funds to purchase equipment for a new mill to be located in Roscommon where Robinson Creek intersects the South Branch. The top subscribers, A. A. Griffin & Ed Kiely each provided $50 while other businessmen provided $25 or 10.

The drive on the Dead Stream will start next week.

May, 1886 – "Construction has begun on the new mill to be operating in Roscommon alongside the South Branch and Robinson Creek. The mill will be 30 by 100 feet long with a 60 hp engine powered by large boilers."

"The Backus Creek dam has burned along with several camp buildings. The dam is the outlet for Mud Lake and is needed by Mr. Boyce and Mr. Langhray for lumbering operations for a job of 5M."

"Mary Starr of Ontario writes requesting information about her husband who was working in the woods. She fears her husband may have been killed while in the woods. The husband left some money in the bank which the wife cannot obtain until the missing man is found or proof of his death is obtained. Anyone having information concerning this matter should contact Mrs. Starr."

The local news in *The Roscommon News* was a mixture of fact, opinion and hearsay yet the stories provide a clue to the general moral standards of the time. They were written in a chatty style as if two neighbors were talking over a backyard fence in a kind of shorthand exchange that lacked detail. Here are a few of the brief news items that appeared in the "Local News" category that are telling.

Nov 20, 1885 - "St Helenites want to keep their doors locked and windows fastened (at) nights. There is a man in the village who has a mania for climbing windows and knocking at doors. When asked who is there, he answers, 'It's me, it's me!' "

Jan. 1886 - "The brutal unprovoked murder of young Ramsey Gregory within a few feet of his home and within the hearing of his parents is a sharp reminder to our city that life is not safe where crime goes unpunished." (no other details provided)

May 20, 1886- "Wm Steckert of Cadillac made a pleasant call to The News this week and L. W Knapp of Houghton Lake also visited." (Both were lumbermen)

July 9, 1886 – "Base Ball is exciting this year."

Aug. 6, 1886- "C. Blanchard returned home with 11 new mustangs that he purchased for his livery business." (Two columns later in the same paper it is reported that "Wednesday night six of Blanchard's mustangs broke out of the pasture."

Feb. 18, 1887- "Mr. Spence Kane was noticed by your correspondent taking a stroll Sunday with two of the prettiest girls this town can boast of."

Mar. 4, 1887- "Mrs. L Carrick proved herself an unnatural mother by last week attempting to desert her husband and 3 children, the youngest being but a year and 4 months old. She became enamored with a man named Kelly who, when he learned the feeling with which he was regarded and the citizens intended to take law into their own hands and punish him, he fled to parts unknown. The husband father came here and the children from near Houghton Lake where the family resided. Sheriff Macklin brought the misguided mother here and the family started back to Ohio on Tuesday where they formerly resided."

May 25, 1887- " Monday night the Rev. O. Barfald was in the village and took a train for other fields. He had been pastor of a church in Cheney where he and his family resided, but hearing that his flock proposed investigating his relations with a Miss Ellen Lewis before her arrival here, he sent his wife to her parents. Miss Lewis left at the same time."

Such was the newspaper that folks in the boom town of Roscommon and the outlying areas of the county read in 19th century. The paper did a creditable job in reporting on national, state and local news as well as providing businesses the opportunity to promote their wares. The standards of the time are reflected in the editor's choice of topics and language in describing affairs that he considered newsworthy. It wasn't an easy job to keep a county informed and make a profit at the same time as the Ward Brothers were able to do for many years. Fortunately, the laws and customs of the time allowed the editor wide discretion in his reporting and little risk of consequent legal action as can be concluded by this last entry.

Jan 1890 "Scott Buell, at one time a village official in Au Sable, and two years ago a candidate for sheriff, is charged with having robbed Scanlon's saloon in Oscoda of $350.00 The charge is based on information of John Nolan who says he was interested in the affair. Nolan, however, is crazy from drink at present."

Chapter 14

Not Everyone Left

Lumberman Henry Stephens senior gradually passed his business to his sons, Henry Jr. and Albert, and senior retired to California in poor health, where he passed away in 1884. By 1894 the timber all around St. Helen had been cut and the Stephens Co. shut down their operations. They dismantled their mills and sent the equipment to other locations, tore down their business office and homes, salvaging what they could for other operations. St. Helen was badly shaken by the sudden loss of business. Only a shadow of its former self, the little town became a virtual ghost town with only five small homes, a railroad station and a school house.

St. Helen's plight and that of Richfield Township was not unique. The entire county was feeling the pain of losing the lumber business. Starting in 1886 lumbering had begun a slow, steady, downward spiral as the forests around the county were used up. Certainly the logging business between 1885 and 1890 was still important to the area and the newspaper continued to report on the comings and goings of lumbermen, although with less frequency and less enthusiasm.

Jan 29, 1886 – "W. J. Terney says there will be in the neighborhood of 12 M feet put in Higgins Lake this season for Muskegon. Rumor has it that C. Blanchard will do the driving."

July 2, 1886 –"The Roscommon Lumber logging road (railroad) from Houghton Lake is now connected to The Flint and Pere Marquette."

Sept 10, 1886 – "B. C. Geel arrived with 10 teams of horses and about 75 men. It is reported that he will have 2 camps and put in 10M on the Au Sable."

Oct 22, 1886 – "The Moore Company is operating on the Au Sable and will put in 21 M as follows: Terney, 5M on the South Branch, Geel, 10 M on the mainstream, Jno Cole, 2M Mainstream, Dan Chalker, 2M on North Branch, Dan McDonald, 2M main stream."

Nov 19, 1886 – "Salling-Hansen has 10 camps, each with 30 -35 men. They will put in 30 M this winter – 2 camps in Grayling, 3 on Otsego Lake, 2 on the Au Sable, 2 on the Manistee."

The Salling-Hansen Co. and the Hansen-Michelson Co. were to Crawford County as The Stephens Co. was to Roscommon County. By far and away they were the largest lumbering firm in Crawford and several of their operations were in the village of Grayling. Like Stephens they owned land, cut and transported logs, sawed and planed lumber so that it was ready for shipment to retail or wholesale customers.

The Roscommon News spoke of their operations with its usual brevity in a manner that seemed almost wistful. "Salling-Hansen owns the big mill in Grayling and they will bank around 90M."- **Feb 12, 1886**

Hansen Planning Mill in Grayling Area

Lumber for Shipment from Grayling
(The train car at the end is barely visible amongst the stacks)

As the decade worn on the newspaper had fewer and fewer reports of lumbering and the names of many of the big lumber operators were absent. The firms of Blodgett and Byrne, A. W. Wright, and the Ducey Lumber Co. for example, were no longer a topic of intense interest. Most of the big operators had fled the county by the end of the decade leaving a gaping hole in the economy.

Business in the county and villages became smaller and smaller. Folks in the area became aware of the change and some, even those only marginally in the lumber business, decided it was time to move on.
"L. W. Knapp, Supervisor of Roscommon Township, advises that his family will move to King County, Washington, where he has bought 160 acres, where 7 M of pine are." Roscommon News, **May 22, 1891**

The big lumbering operations moved quietly from the county to areas further north and west. Those lumber men that remained continued cutting the remaining forest stands but it was clear the large volume work done just a few years before would never be repeated. Much of the remaining lumbering was done to satisfy local markets and smaller saw mills. The large mills at the Michigan coastal areas in Muskegon and Oscoda began to rely on logs towed to them from further and further distances. Some could no longer compete and so they discontinued operations.

The big drives down the rivers became fewer and fewer. On the Au Sable, the river that had seen millions of logs floating downriver each year, big drives became a thing for memories. The last large drive was conducted by a man from the village of McKinley, J. H. Harp Hayes. Hayes organized a drive in 1896 when he and 40 other men spent 90 days escorting logs from McKinley to the mouth of the river and saw mills located there. It was the last large drive ever on the Au Sable.

The county was further offended by forest fires that occurred with regularity in the wake of the lumbering operations. When the lumbermen took the logs they wanted they left slash, everything from the trees except the sought-after logs. The accumulated needles, leaves and branches were left lying exactly as they fell, creating a huge reservoir of kindling and brush for fires. The prevailing opinion during that time was that nothing could be done to prevent or control forest fires. When a fire began for whatever reason, the town folks and rural farmers watched helplessly, hoping that the wind or the rain would save their homes from devastation.

It was only a matter of good luck that prevented a major Roscommon catastrophe from the fires. Other counties and towns in northern Michigan weren't so lucky. Fires swept through many areas after the lumbermen left and millions of acres of Michigan were burned over. The twin towns of Oscoda and Au Sable were two of the unlucky towns; a fire swept through the both towns in 1911 and nearly burned both to extinction. Only 20 buildings were left in Oscoda and Au Sable had even fewer. The fire was called the worst ever in Michigan.

One of the few things that provided an economic boost to the area was one of the most unlikely; the picking and marketing of huckleberries. Huckleberries, the small blue-black berries that grew wild in the forest areas had been known in the area for thousands of years as local Indians counted them among the fruits of the forest that they consumed. Early visitors to the area called them 'whortleberries.' These wild berries, although tiny, grew in the sandy upland soil and the burnt areas of the forest further stimulated their growth. The result was Roscommon people began picking them for delivery by the railroad to distant markets.

An active market developed for the delicious tiny berries. First they were sold by the quart and then, almost amazingly, by the bushel. Migrant workers came to Roscommon to camp in the woods and pick the berries as well as local folks who had the time available for picking.

Godrey Hirzel's Camp for the Buying of Huckleberries
(Note the Indian children on the table under the tent) –Photo from Gerrish Township Centennial publication

The Roscommon News began noting the prices and shipments of huckleberries. They said that the total shipments in 1885 amounted to 4,000 bushels at a value of $6,000. Despite worries to the contrary, the crop in 1886 was even better as reported by *The News.*

July 13, 1886 - "Huckleberries are scarce this year and merchants are paying 6 cents a quart. The first bushel was shipped out."

Aug20, 1886 - "9,000 bushels of huckleberries shipped at $1.50 each."

The other county businesses that were not related to lumbering were the tourist trade and paradoxically, the shipment of vension from the area. Tourism to the county had been a small, but significant part of county business since its inception. The Michigan Central Railroad did its part to encourage tourism since nearly all tourists rode the train (or the cars in the vernacular of the time) to come to the area. Tourists who came to the county did so for the same reasons then as now – to enjoy the wilderness areas and the lakes and streams, and to pursue the taking of game and fish.

Roscommon County was still home to large numbers of wildlife during these days. The newspaper reported on the problems with bears plaguing the lumber camps in the remote areas and one story detailed how a woman in Cheboygan barely escaped an attack of wild wolves as she ventured a dozen steps from her home. Fortunately, she was carrying her revolver and she put it to good use. These reports of abundant wildlife brought sportsmen to the area.

Higgins and Houghton Lakes had been a tourist draw since the beginning and the Au Sable was known far and wide for fishing. Deer hunting was also a draw then as now. The most famous of the fish was the Grayling, the abundant, easy to catch trout that fishermen talked about from Michigan to the east coast of the United States.

Grayling trout and whitetail deer were plentiful enough so that both were taken from Roscommon forests and the Au Sable and shipped on the railroad in regular commerce. Like the logging operations, no one paid any particular attention to the numbers taken based on the assumption they would always be available no matter the havoc to the environment occurring everywhere nearby. The Grayling trout was ultimately 'fished out' in the Au Sable, never to return.

Of the major lumbermen, only Nels Michelson would continue lumbering operations on the west side of Houghton Lake after the turn of the century; all the others had either left or were working at a fraction of their earlier business volumes. When the 19th century ended the townships and villages were so devoid of economic activity that many businesses were forced to move or die.

But not everyone left Roscommon County. A few stalwarts stayed, including a few lumbermen, who had made a living harvesting the pines. These were those who fell in love with the area, who stayed on to work and make progress through the harder times after the boom was over. Three men who represented that class were Charles Blanchard, William Terney and Peter Pruden. Each had done much to settle the area and make it work and each stayed after the barons left and much of the timber was gone.

Pruden was in one of the early waves of settlers to come to Roscommon County. He was different than most settlers; in fact he was different than most men as he navigated his life to a frontier area after most would have been content to pursue a less arduous life. Ambitious, hard-working and multi-talented, Pruden started more businesses and succeeded more often than most men dream about.

Peter W. Pruden was born in 1826 in New York to a family that ultimately included 10 children. The family moved west in a series of moves and finally ended up in southern Michigan in Ionia, between Lansing and Grand Rapids where Peter's father, Boyer, died in 1855. By then, the 27 year-old Peter had married Catherine, had sired one daughter, Ella, and had moved to a nearby village in the same county.

When the Civil War broke out in 1861, Pruden, at age 34 was a middle-aged man by the standards of the time. The war effort and his patriotism must have weighed heavily on Pruden because he enlisted as a Private at age 36 to face the terrors of war leaving behind his spouse and his then 11 year old daughter. Peter performed well in the army and was promoted to full Sergeant in August, 1865 as a member of the 1st Engineers Regiment, Michigan. The war ended soon thereafter and Peter was mustered out in September in Nashville, TN.

He made his way back to Michigan and resumed his life in a new village in the same county that he had left. After 1870, Pruden decided to take advantage of the government's offer to provide free land for farming and he ended up as a neighbor to the Denton's in Denton Township, Roscommon County. Like the Denton's, Peter took an active role in the formation of the township and county serving in various capacities (see Chapter 8).

Since it must have seemed that everyone in the county was involved in logging and lumbering in some way, Pruden soon concentrated on that business instead of farming. He and another neighbor, Dresdan Bryan, became partners and built a saw mill along the shores of Houghton Lake. Pruden was active in running the mill and he hired others to help in cutting and skidding logs as fodder for his mill. Before long, Pruden decided to take advantage of the growing need for lodging among lumbermen and other visitors to the area and so he built a large frame structure, one of the first hotels in the area. The resulting village that grew around his hotel and mill was known first as Edna and later as Prudenville. Again, Pruden was a 'hands-on' manager as he operated the hotel and its large restaurant.

As the Roscommon lumbering era was drawing to a close in 1890 and Pruden was a 64 year-old, he continued to live on in Roscommon County. He had been one of the first settlers and political office-holders of the county, serving in a variety of township positions including postmaster. His resume would have noted that he was an early logger, one of the few local residents to build and own a saw mill and a hotel with a first class restaurant. He managed the hotel and restaurant and also became owner of a general store. It was noted that Pruden was an unfailing supporter of all things local, providing his help and support for many local projects. He left Roscommon at an advanced age as poor health overtook him. He died in Bay City when he was 86 years old.

One of Pruden's peers was a younger man, though no less ambitious. He was Charles Blanchard, a young man who came to Roscommon County in 1875 whereupon he promptly opened a store in the new village of the Roscommon Station. A few years later he opened a livery business that became a long term operation that served the interests of a large clientele of travelers who needed transportation after arriving on the train. Blanchard also began a varied career in the lumber business and he took on many other business endeavors including those in the political arena. He built a splendid home and spent his entire life in the village of Roscommon dying there in 1924. His esteem in the village and county was widespread as his life touched many others over his varied career and he unswervingly supported the growth and development of Roscommon County.

Charles Blanchard was born on a farm near Brooklyn, Jackson County, Michigan 1854 and he grew there as a member of the Blanchard family with 10 children. He came north to Roscommon County and established a store in the village of Roscommon when he was about 20 years old. After a few years as a store-keeper, Blanchard opened a livery business that became a life-long preoccupation. His horses, stage and buggies for rent or hire were the principal means for travel for those exiting the train station that had land to look over or camps to visit, or some other important business elsewhere in the county. Blanchard used his livery business to advantage as he began a stage line that provided regular trips to Higgins Lake for those who camped at Lakeside, Cottage Grove or Pinewoods.

He married Catherine Haley in 1878 and the two produced three children before Nov. 1883 when Catherine passed away. In Dec. of 1885 he re-married, this time to Elizabeth Murphy from Simcoe, Canada. Charles and Elizabeth also produced three children during their marriage.

Blanchard joined forces with two other men, John Coleman of Roscommon and T. E. Douglas of Grayling to begin manufacture of lumber and barrel staves at St. Helen. Their firm, the Blanchard, Coleman & Company, purchased a tract of timber land to supply the mill and they ran this business for several years.

Blanchard also ventured on his own in the lumber business and signed a contract with another firm, the Handy Brothers of Bay City, to provide Jack Pine and sunken logs reclaimed from the river. He also operated modest-sized lumber camps as a jobber providing logs for mills at the mouth of the Muskegon River. He took on various lumbering jobs around the county including the job of 'driving' lumber across Higgins Lake to the Cut River. He also had a saw mill of his own near Higgins Lake that produced lumber for both local consumption and long distance shipping via Michigan Central from Roscommon Station. The lumber that he produced for local consumption was sold at Blanchard's store.

Newspaper Advertising for Blanchard's Roscommon Store in April 1922

His business interests were varied. One venture that must have been profitable for many years was a gravel business. Blanchard had purchased land 3 miles north of Roscommon where lay thousands of tons of sand and gravel that Blanchard sold to the railroad. The railroad installed their own spur to Blanchard's gravel pit to pick loads for their many uses.

Along with the gravel business, Blanchard became involved in road building for an interurban (a railroad for passenger travel between cities). In 1901, he took a job of constructing an interurban road between Detroit and Ann Arbor and later he built a portion of another railroad north of Bay City. His credits include the building of the first gravel road in Roscommon County.

Roscommon County was the host to several Blanchard's. The newspaper reported on the death of one John Blanchard who "was instantly killed by a falling limb in the Pack & Woods lumber camp" in November of 1886. Charles' brother Arthur and his wife managed the Pioneer House in 1887 while Charles' mother, also named Elizabeth, lived with Charles and his family. She passed away in May of 1891 after living in Roscommon for 14 years.

The Pioneer House (now known as Spruce Motor Lodge)

The same month of May saw Charles called to his saw mill near Higgins Lake on an emergency basis. One of the forest fires that was raging in the area came close to his mill and Charles mustered a group to help fight the fire that saved his mill.

As he matured, Blanchard felt the call of public service and he began a 10 year political career that saw him serve four years as County Sheriff, four years as County Treasurer, and two years as Register of Deeds. He also served as a member of the school board, the village council and as President of the village.

He continued his businesses while serving in public office including his retail sale of lumber at a store in Roscommon and he kept an office in the village as well. He remained healthy until the last year of his life at which time old age crept up on him restricting his activities somewhat. Finally, in the spring of 1922 he died. His funeral at his home was said to be one of the largest ever held in Roscommon with visitors from Detroit, Bay City, Lansing, Grayling, Rose City and elsewhere.

The Chas. Blanchard Home on Lake Street in Roscommon

The last of our three stalwart Roscommon citizens to be reviewed is William J. Terney, lumberman. Terney's career and contributions to the county echo those of both Pruden with his Civil War experience and Blanchard with his public service. Terney was born in 1847 in Michigan to a family of Irish immigrants. He married in 1869 at age 22 to a girl of Irish heritage, Sarah Ann Mallory. The two lived where the young William earned a living like many others; as a farmer in southern Michigan. When the Civil War began, William joined the 3rd Michigan Regiment, 3 Michigan Cavalry as an enlisted man with the rank of Private. After the war was over, Terney headed north to make a living as a lumberman.

Terney worked as a jobber contracting to "put in" logs for the large firm of Moore and Whipple. His camp was near the South Branch of Au Sable, north of St. Helen. He made his headquarters at St. Helen but kept his home and family downstate, making regular trips home during the warmer months when the logging season was over in late April.

The *Roscommon News* kept regular tabs on his work although they occasionally misspelled his name:

" W. J. Terney is lumbering 4 miles north of St Helen and has 5M on skids which will go into the Au Sable."

"W. J. Terney of Port Huron has gone to Geel's Landing with 16 men to put in 4.5 M for Moore. There will be a 1.5 mile haul to the Au Sable."

"W. J. Tierney finished up his job down the railroad some 7 miles south of this place. He reported great results: no sickness and 4 M put in. He is contemplating a dray haul and should he undertake it, he may move his family to Roscommon."

"W Terney, an old jobber for Moore and Whipple is lumbering near Roscommon with plans for putting in 3 MM."

By 1887 most of the big pines were cut along the South Branch so Terney and his men continued work by logging other trees that didn't command quite the same price as the pine but were still valuable. Again the newspaper reported, "Terney is lumbering on the South Branch and is putting in dry hemlock – April, 1887". By this time Terney had his family with him and he decided to move to the village of Roscommon. He began by first renting a house at the same site where he would subsequently build a permanent home, the corner of Lake and 7th street. His elegant home was richly appointed with parquet oak floors and ornate paneling that was the talk of the town when it was built. Sadly, Sarah lived only a few years in her new home before she died in 1904, leaving William a widower, a status that he maintained the rest of his life.

The William Terney House in 2011 (photo by the author)

(William Terney built this Queen Anne style house in the village of Roscommon after 1887. The elaborate porch with the contrasting paint highlights a common architectural feature of Victorian era homes in many areas.)

In 1900 William and Sarah Terney were 52 years old, living in Roscommon with a single border as a replacement for the children who had all left home by this time. With the lumbering era all but disappeared, William decided to engage in the real estate business. His work and dealings with county officials soon led him to enter politics as well. He found it to his liking and folks seemed to be comfortable having him as one of their leaders. He was appointed as County Treasurer first and then elected as Village President in 1904.

Terney continued in the real estate business throughout the rest of his life selling lots on Higgins Lake and other properties around the county. He lived in Michelson in 1926 and was active until the end when he left Roscommon for a brief period to convalesce at his brother's home at Smith Creek. He died there at age 79, having lived in Roscommon for the previous 40 years.

Pruden, Blanchard and Terney were all pioneers of Roscommon County and each took advantage of the richest resource in the area, the forests, to earn a living in the remote area. As lumbermen, each was successful along with scores of others who lumbered in the area. Unlike other lumbermen who came to Roscommon in search of riches and then left, Pruden, Blanchard and Terney stayed on through thick and thin. Roscommon County was by far richer for having these three stay when much of the forest had been taken by the turn of the century. It was indeed a good thing that not everyone left, especially talented men like these three.

Chapter 15

Savior of the County

The entire County was in dire straits in 1902. Local business men had known it was coming for some time as they watched their businesses dwindle year after year as the logging operations came to a halt. It seemed there was no good reason to stay in the county after the main economic engine, logging and lumber- making, had slowed to a trickle compared to the former waterfall. With most lumber camps gone, the farmers had no ready market for their produce without the high cost of shipping. Cash flow throughout the entire area dried up and people started moving to other areas in search of economic opportunities. Those who moved were unable to sell their land as there were no buyers – most just left, leaving in their wake unpaid tax bills.

The largest offenders in unpaid taxes were the largest land owners, the lumber barons who had stripped the land of its riches. Not only did some fail to make good for the original purchase of the land, they also failed to pay their yearly taxes. Even the respected Henry Stephens Co. hadn't paid their tax bill for the last two years. And Roscommon County was not alone. By the early 20th century, 1,000,000 acres of land in Oscoda, Iosco, Ogemaw, and Alcona had returned to government ownership because of non-payment of taxes.

At the beginning of the 20th century, Roscommon County had little to no income; suddenly county government seemed unable to operate and the State of Michigan was biting at their heels. The assessed valuation of each township had fallen like an anchor to the bottom of Higgins Lake. By 1902 the situation seemed at rock bottom and the State seemed to think there was nothing to be done for it other than having County Government close up shop. The State felt this was a practical solution since three quarters of county land was already tax delinquent: Of course, the Commissioners felt otherwise and dug in their heels to prevent the State from taking over. The State Land Commission considered stripping the County of its remaining assets; the standing timber left on some parcels of land. Further, a bill had been crafted in the State Legislature to incorporate all or part of Roscommon County into a new state entity to be known as The Higgins Lake State Forest – would Roscommon County disappear, perhaps forever? The County Board responded by asking the County Prosecutor to decide if legal action could be pursued to thwart the Land Commission.

In May of 1902, things had pretty much come to a head and the County Board of Supervisors were having emergency meetings day after day and on weekends to decide on a course of action. One avenue the Board took was issuing a letter to the Governor signed by all County Commissioners arguing their case. The letter was prepared with great care and the Commissioners used the argument that a State takeover would spoil the potential for agriculture in the county. The Board took up a familiar argument: that the county had an unfair reputation of being a poor place to raise crops when, in fact, the Commissioners said, Roscommon County was an above average place for agriculture. (Of course, the Commissioners had no facts and no basis for making such a claim.) The Governor didn't respond to the argument.

Into this mix of activity a stranger suddenly appeared and he made it known that he had an idea that he wanted to talk over with the Board. The stranger was unknown to the Board, but when he explained that he was interested in buying large quantities of Roscommon land, the Board decided now would be a good time to listen to the man from Chicago who had traveled all the way to north central Michigan to talk with them.

John Carter taken around 1915

The handsome stranger was a youngish, well-dressed man named John Carter. In the preceding weeks, unbeknownst to the Board, Carter had been quietly investigating the possibilities for real estate investments in Roscommon County and he learned about the depressed prices and the lands for sale. Carter made a bold proposal to the Board, would they offer tax rebates if he would promise to put properties back on the tax roll? Carter explained that he had his eye on Henry Stephens Co. property, a solid block of 144,000 acres, more than a third of the entire county. If he could entice Stephens to sell at a reasonable price, he promised to pay the back taxes on the property. The Board was nearly dumbfounded. They readily agreed to Carter's proposal with a proviso: the state had set a deadline of 10 days for some payments due; Carter had to come up with funds in time to pay. Carter agreed and the race was on.

Carter left town that night on the outgoing train for his home in Chicago to begin raising the needed cash. The Board sent word to Lansing that something was afoot that offered hope for the salvation of the county. For several days the anxious Board members waited. Then, with one day remaining before the ten day deadline, a smiling Carter returned to Roscommon on the Michigan Central. He had raised the needed money. He had met with friends and former Chicago business associates who furnished the capital in exchange for a share of the expected profits. Carter explained to the Board of Supervisors about the money he had raised and headed for a meeting with Albert and Henry Stephens concerning the 144,000 acre tract.

At first, the brothers held out for an exorbitant price. When Carter explained his agreement with the Board of Supervisors and the fact that the Stephens Company would be penalized by a doubling of their delinquent taxes if they wanted to hold on to the property, they finally agreed to a reasonable price. Within a few weeks of their handshake, Carter returned to the County as the Chief Officer of the St. Helen Development Company and the deed to the 144,000 acres changed hands - John Carter was now in control of the largest block of property in Roscommon County.

Carter had a big job in front of him. The slowdown and eventual end of the lumbering era hit the county especially hard. Without the numerous lumbering camps and the many jacks invading the towns and the saw mills sitting quiet or tore down, there just wasn't enough economic activity to support everyone even though the population had fallen off. Farmers who had previously sold hay to the camps for the horses and produce for the jacks now had no local market. The population of the county declined precipitously. In 1904 the population was listed at just over 2,000 people total with the village of Roscommon reporting a total of 407 souls – a decline of 50% for the village.

Seven townships reported the following population figures:

Denton	82	Gerrish	182
Higgins	535	Markey	80
Nester	202	Roscommon	305
Richfield	288		

The settlements that had once dotted the county were also drying up and some had already become ghost towns by 1904. As the people left the tiny settlements of Geels, Moore and others, the signs of their presence slowly faded as the buildings burned or were torn down and the well-worn paths and trails marking their presence faded away. None of that discouraged the young, energetic Carter.

Carter was a superb salesman and he had a plan. His plan was to market the land in Roscommon to folks in the big cities, starting with Chicago. He calculated that he could sell off land from the huge tracts by marketing smaller parcels as farms, and in doing so, generate substantial profits. If the land to be sold had soil that wasn't suitable for raising crops, why then the buyers could raise livestock. Here was their chance to buy land of their own at depressed prices, according to the salesman Carter.

Carter created The St. Helen Development Company to raise the cash necessary to finance the project. He issued $1000 bonds at 6% interest for investors with the option that investors could elect to receive 40 acres of Roscommon land in lieu of the $1000. Carter added an inducement: the first 100 buyers would receive materials for a house, a barn, one cow, ten sheep, two brood sows and 250 chicks, enough livestock to make most farmers nod their heads in agreement. Carter began a variety of marketing moves to promote land sales including excursions from Chicago to St. Helen to show off the properties. His marketing efforts, like most of the things he undertook, were successful and crowds of people traveled to St. Helen. In one case, Carter sold an entire township of six square miles to a man from Milwaukee.

Passengers Arriving in St. Helen

(Carter organized excursion trains to St. Helen for prospective buyers to examine the lands for sale.)

Carter marketed the area all around St. Helen as an agricultural area. Many of the buyers of Carter's lands were indeed farmers who became successful. Raising chickens and selling eggs developed into a niche business for many who purchased Carter's Roscommon lands. The eggs were shipped by The Michigan Central Railroad all around the country.

John Carter was easily the most successful real estate developer in Roscommon County. Through his efforts, the County avoided default on its financial obligations. Carter promoted St. Helen and Richfield Township for many years and he built an attractive home near the lake where he and his family resided despite his many trips to Chicago and elsewhere. He retained title to more than 2,000 acres of Richfield Township land including a large tract on the north side of Lake St. Helen and most of the section containing Russell Lake that Carter descendants still own.

Eggs Ready for Shipment at the St. Helen Station

John Carter turned out to be the savior of Roscommon County and St. Helen. He provided much needed cash for the county and an economic boost with real estate sales. The influx of farmers who raised crops or livestock or both saved St. Helen and Richfield Township. The area survived and eventually became prosperous for some farmers, especially those that were able to raise livestock for market. The stimulus provided by Carter was enough to help stabilize the entire county as other areas in the county began to slowly recover from the loss of the major lumber operations.

[John Carter also provided the area with another famous and valuable legacy: he was the grandfather of the renowned Hollywood actor Charlton Heston.

Charlton Heston in 1950

Heston won The Oscar for Best Actor for his performance in Ben Hur at the 32nd Academy Awards

Charlton Heston (1923 – 2008) grew up around St. Helen with his mother and father, Russell Carter, son of John Carter and mother Lilla Charlton . When he was ten years old his parents divorced and his mother subsequently married a man named Chester Heston who adopted the young boy who thereupon took the name Charlton Heston. Heston said he decided to become an actor after his St. Helen school teacher gave him a part in the Christmas play at age five.

Charlton Heston was an important symbol for Roscommon County. Those county residents who knew of him and his growing up in St. Helen were justifiably proud of his accomplishments. He returned periodically to the area where he grew up and spent time with his boyhood acquaintances and family members. The things that rubbed off on him from his youth in Roscommon stayed with him, he continued to be a sportsman and lover of the outdoors for the rest of his life.]

And so this story of the early history of Roscommon County comes to an end with the beginning work of John Carter, a master salesman and superlative real estate developer. Carter's success was due in part to the extraordinary environment of the county. Roscommon County's environment has been shaped by the forces of nature over the last 4.5 billion years. Its topography, soil, and flora were all determined by powerful geological forces. These geologic forces occurred over several billion years in a landscape that was devoid of humans for most of its history. The result of nature's play on the county is beautiful lakes, powerful and plentiful streams, and both dry and wet areas that are home to uncountable numbers of diverse wildlife.

The wild animals were the draw for the first humans that came to Roscommon. The number of these first inhabitants was small and probably all were transient, traveling across the area in the chase for meat. They were replaced by other humans who were able to provide a slightly more comfortable life for themselves as they developed a variety of stone tools for their use. Their numbers were also small - no more than a few hundred would have lived in the county at any one time.

This second wave of humans lived in Roscommon for several thousand years. They left evidence of their lives at all three of the large lakes in the county and at other sites as well. We don't know what names they used for themselves neither are we certain where these inhabitants came from nor went as their records are in stone only. It was not until white men appeared in the county, perhaps in the late 17th century, that written records were created and names were given. "Indians," they were called as early Frenchmen perpetuated the error begun by Christopher Columbus.

First the French, then English and finally Americans became interested in Roscommon land for the pelts of the creatures that lived here. A trade developed in these pelts that lasted until something even more important took over, the logging business. Roscommon and all of northern Michigan became the focus of attention as logging moved northward from Saginaw.

By the time the forests in Roscommon were assaulted for their bounty, the loggers had become adept at cutting and removing the timber and so most of Roscommon's forests were denuded in a brief 25 year period.

The logging business provoked the development of the county with a wave of immigrants who came to earn a living. As the lumbering era came to an end, many of those who came left. But not everyone. Those who remained and those who came after the logging era were the hardy folks who helped transform a raw and sometimes wild area into a civilized place as nature began to heal the wounds inflicted by the logging operations.

Those of us who live here in the 21st century are the recipients of an area that was settled, tamed and transfigured by the earliest settlers. They made roads, drew maps, built bridges, and brought a measure of civilization to a remote area. We owe them much for having done their part in opening up this beautiful area for us. The least we can do is understand what they did during THE EARLY HISTORY OF ROSCOMMON COUNTY.

You may exit the time travel vehicle by turning the last page.

THE END

Bibliography

A History of Lakeside Association, Arthur W. Rosenau, Lakeside Association, 1979

A memoir of Roscommon, Michigan, James H. Curnalia (undated)

A Winter in the Pine Woods, C. A. Wean, Chicago, 1899

An Introduction to the History of the Grayling Area, 3rd edition, 1999

Archeology of Michigan, Wilbert B. Hinsdale, University of Michigan, Ann Arbor, 1931

Capsules of Time, Beulah Carman, Houghton Lake, Michigan, 1987

Carl Addison Leech Collection, Roscommon Notes, Bentley Historical Library, University of Michigan

David Shoppenagon and The Place Between the Rivers, W.E. Tudor, Roscommon, 2008

Geology of Michigan, John Dorr & Donald Eschman, the University of Michigan Press, Ann Arbor, 1971

Gerrish Township Centennial, Ivan S. Willett, et. al., 1980

Great Lakes Archaeology, Ronald Mason, Academic Press, 1981

Historical Aspects of the Village of Roscommon, Ned Curtis, 1975 (CMU paper)

Historic Women of Michigan, Keith Widder, reprinted in Mackinac History Volume IV, 2007

History of Saginaw County, Volume II, James Cook Mills, Saginaw Mi, 1918(digitized by Google)

History of Michigan, Volume 2, Charles Moore, Chicago, 1915

Bibliography

Indian Life in the Upper Great Lakes, George I. Quimby, University of Chicago Press, 1960

Looking Back, A Centennial History of Houghton Lake, Beulah Carman, 1979

Michigan Ghost Towns, Volume II, Roy L Dodge, Sterling Heights, Mi. 1971

Michigan Rogues Desperados Cutthroats, Tom Powers, Holt Michigan, 2002

Michigan State Business Gazatteer and Business Directory, R. L. Polk & Co., various dates

Private Conversation, Dr. Jim Sullivan, Houghton Lake, Oct 21, 2010

Private Correspondence, Martin Rosenson, April, 2011

Retrieving Michigan's Buried Past: The Archeology of the Great Lakes State, John R. Halsey, Cranbrook Institute of Science, 1999

Roscommon Magazine, V 3 No. 3, Dan Fishel, 2006

Roscommon County Centennial, 1875 – 1975, Historical Committee: James Curnalia et al, 1975

The Heritage of Richfield Township St. Helen, Peggy Diss, Roscommon, MI, 1976

The History of Northern Michigan, Perry F. Powers, Chicago, 1912

The Archeology of Michigan, James E. Fitting, The American Museum of Natural History, The Natural History Press, Garden City, New York

The City of Detroit, Michigan, 1701 – 1922, edited by Burton, Stocking and Miller, Volume 3

Bibliography

The First 100 Years, An Introduction to the History of the Grayling Area, The Crawford County Avalanche, 1972

The Michigan Fur Trade, Ida Amanda Johnson, Lansing, Michigan Historical Commission, 1919

The Story of Man, Cyril Aydon, N.Y., N. Y., 2007

The White Pine Industry and the Transformation of 19th Century Michigan, Mark Neithercut, U of M Doctoral Thesis, 1974

Upper Tittabawassee River Boom Towns, Stan Berriman, Midland Mi., 1971

Wikipedia and numerous internet sites with a connection to Roscommon history

Index of Names Important to Roscommon

Index of Names Important to Roscommon